BEEMER'S TALE

How a Shelter Rescue Became a Certified Therapy Dog

By

M. Sacko

Copyright © 2019 M.Sacko. All rights reserved.
Published by M.Sacko

ISBN 978-0-578-21628-7

All rights reserved. No parts of this book may be reproduced or transmitted in any form or by any means, electronically or mechanical, including photocopying, recording or by any information storage or retrieval system without permission from the author, except for the quotations in a review.

This book is a work of nonfiction. Certain names and identifying characteristics have been changed.

Cover Background Photo by [Redd Angelo](#) on [Unsplash](#)

The proceeds of Beemer's Tale will be donated to local shelters and used to help support Pet Adoption and Pet Therapy.

For Thee "Best Boy in the World and Handsomest Guy in Town" – Beautiful Beemer.

On all our car rides you were Always our "Wingman".

Thank you for your Service to Others and Being the Joy in our Life Every Day.

One of a Kind. Once in a Lifetime. Priceless.

Table of Contents

Prologue – Fall 2001 1

Chapter 1 – The Meeting 2

Chapter 2 – Adoption 9

Chapter 3 – Growing Up 17

Chapter 4 – Welcome Home 25

Chapter 5 – Daily Life – Part 1 29

Chapter 6 – Training 60

Chapter 7 – Friends and Family – Part 1 85

Chapter 8 – Parks, Parades and Parties – Part 1 . . . 110

Chapter 9 – Grooming 134

Chapter 10 – Food – Anything Goes 142

Chapter 11 – Therapy Visits – Part 1 147

Chapter 12 – Allergies and Diet 176

Chapter 13 – Crossing Over 180

Chapter 14 – Weather 189

Chapter 15 – Fun with Beemer 199

Chapter 16 – Daily Life – Part 2 234

Chapter 17 – Parks, Parades and Parties – Part 2 . . 272

Chapter 18 – Friends and Family – Part 2 296

Chapter 19 – Therapy Visits – Part 2 309

Chapter 20 – Holistic Healing and Medication 334

Chapter 21 – Food – The Enemy 347

Chapter 22 – Last Leg 353

Chapter 23 – Reward and Retirement 365
Chapter 24 – Walk On 379
Post Author's Note 382
Timeline – Highlights 383
Tribute 389
Acknowledgements 394

Prologue – Fall 2001

He was found by the side of the road alone with a broken leg. He was just a puppy.

He was taken to the closest shelter. No one came looking for him or reported him missing. The shelter gave him medical attention and his leg healed.

He lived at the shelter for six months. His only view of the world every day was through a metal gate.

No one adopted him and then one day…

Chapter 1 – The Meeting

One Spring day in April 2002 the phone rang. It was early Saturday morning. Looking at the Caller ID I saw it was our friend Rob.

"Hey Rob how are you?"

"Hey. I am thinking of getting Bobby a dog and am going to the shelter today."

"Wow really? Does he want one?" I was so excited.

"I think it would be good for him."

"Aww that would be great. Can I come?" I asked. "I would love to see the puppies."

"Yeah sure. That's why I'm calling. I thought it would be good to have another opinion. We are going in about an hour so we will swing by and pick you up."

"Great! See you soon."

"Later." Rob's usual response as he hung up.

I went to the bedroom to see if Jack was awake. His eyes were slightly open. "Guess where we are going?" I said cheerfully.

"I heard." He groaned.

"Oh come on. It will be fun. Get up and get dressed. I will get your coffee. We leave in an hour."

Right on time Rob pulled up with his son Bobby in what Rob called 'The Beast.' It was a Royal Blue Dodge Ram Truck with Monster Truck wheels. You could hear it rumble from up the street. Rob parked in front of our house and stepped out of the truck. Rob is a big sturdy guy with short dark hair, cut military style, and piercing blue eyes. His expression is always serious but looks like he is up to something whenever he smiles. Very different from Jack who is a little shorter and lean with brown eyes and wears glasses. Many people say Jack looks like a state trooper. Jack actually was a volunteer with the Special Police for several years before we were married. The only thing Rob and Jack have in common look wise is that they both have short dark hair. This is totally opposite of me with long blonde hair.

I burst out the door. I am so happy to be going with them. I walk over to the truck. I had to stand on tip toes as I am only 5'2" and the truck is so high.

"Hi Bobby – how are you?"

Bobby answers with a quiet "Good." Bobby is very tall and thin with light brown hair.

"Jack should be out in a minute. They say women take long to get ready but he is always the last one out." I say to Rob.

Rob just shakes his head and grins.

I clap my hands and say "So where are we going?"

"Thought we would try the shelter in Southton. It's about twenty minutes from here."

"Sounds good." I turn to Bobby. "So are you excited?"

"Yeah I guess so." Bobby replied.

Beemer's Tale 4

Out walks Jack. We get into the truck and are on our way.

As we pulled up to the facility we knew we were in the right place as we could hear barking. We went inside and Rob said "We are here to look at dogs for adoption."

The woman at the counter said "Hold on. Someone will be out in a minute to take you around." She called on the phone and asked someone to come out front.

An older lady, thin with short gray hair comes out from behind the counter. She was dressed in a sweater, jeans and sneakers.

"Hi I am Jane."

"I am Rob and this is my son Bobby."

"Hi. I am Louann and this is my husband Jack."

"So Bobby are you ready to have a new friend?" Jane asked.

Bobby nodded.

"Let's go out back to the ones outside first." When we get outside she said "Feel free to walk down. Let me know if you see any you are interested in."

We made our way down the cages. Reading the tags and looking at the dogs. I looked at the one tag and it said 'Sweet Pea.'

"Aww maybe Sweet Pea is the one." I leaned forward to look in and see a large Shepherd Mix. "Hi Sweet Pea." The dog lunged toward the gate with a loud bark. "Whoa." I instantly backed up. "I guess Sweet Pea maybe isn't so sweet after all." We all laughed.

As we made our way down the cages we saw they were all mostly older dogs. Not that there is anything wrong with that but Rob was interested in one a little younger for Bobby. We walked back over to where Jane was waiting for us. "So did you see any you like?" Jane asked.

Rob said "We are looking for a little bit younger dog. Do you have any puppies?"

"Yes we have a few inside. We like to give our older ones a chance first otherwise no one gets to see them."

We followed her inside. Behind the counter there was another row of cages. Halfway down we saw an adorable brindle, brown and black, puppy with long floppy ears. His name was 'Brownie.'

"Oh he is so adorable." I said. We all agreed and then we saw there was a "Hold for Adoption" sign.

"Brownie has several people already lined up for adoption." Jane explained. As we got up from saying goodbye to Brownie I turned and spotted two white feet sticking out under the gate of the last cage. I immediately walked over to see. When I looked, in there was this black puppy lying down with soft brown eyes and semi-erect ears that folded over at the tip. They instantly reminded me of Sister Bertrille from the "Flying Nun." I glanced at the tag 'Lab/Pit Bull mix – male'. The puppy also had a big patch of white on his chest. He just looked up at me. He didn't get up or jump or bark like some of the other dogs did when you came to the gate.

"Hi there." I said softly as I bent down to be eye level. "Oh you are so cute." I got a little wag of his tail. He just kept looking. I turned my head toward where Rob, Bobby and Jack were looking at another dog and waved intensely. "Come over here guys." When I looked back I saw the tip of his tail was white just like his feet.

"Look at him. Isn't he cute?" Bobby bent down next to me and Beemer sniffed out through the cage when Bobby held his hand out.

"He seems okay." Rob said. Rob leaned forward to get a better look and read the card. He gave me the eye and said "Lab/Pit Mix huh?"

Bobby broke the stare. "Can we see him Dad?"

Rob stood up straight. "Might as well since we're here." Rob walked toward Jane. "Can we see this one?"

"Of course. Come outside and we can let him out." Jane said.

I was so busy looking at him I forgot to look at what his name was. We went outside and she opened the outside door to the cage. He shot out like a bullet out into the yard.

"Wow he is so fast!" I laughed and turned toward Jane.

"Yes that one loves to run. You would never know he first came here with a broken leg." she said.

"Oh my God really?"

"Yes he was found by the side of the road with a broken leg. He has been here six months."

"Oh my, poor guy. What is his name?"

"They named him 'Beemer'."

"Beemer – that's different. What happened to him?" I asked concerned.

"No one knows. The person who found him was not sure if he wandered off or someone left him there."

When Jane let him out it was obvious Beemer was so happy to be outside. It was so funny to watch him run around with his nose sniffing the ground. He seemed more interested in being outside then in us. When standing in the sun Beemer looked so black and shiny like high gloss. You could see distinctly the white on his chest, four white feet and the tip of his tail was white. He really was adorable. To me he looked more Labish.

I cupped my hands and called to Bobby "His name is Beemer."

Bobby called him over "Beemer - here boy." Beemer ran right by him. We were able to pet him when he stopped to smell something on the ground. Beemer was so soft and his ears felt like velvet.

I walked over to where Rob and Bobby were standing. "So what do you think?"

"Can we get him Dad?" Bobby asked.

Rob rubbed his chin. "I don't know. I think we should keep looking. This is only the first one we've seen."

"Oh man." Bobby whined.

I felt bad when Jane had to call Beemer to go back in his cage.

We thanked Jane. Rob said they were going think about it and would get back to her. We headed back to the truck.

"Well I think he is really cute." I said.

"Yeah well we'll see." Rob replied.

"Dad don't you think we should take him before someone else does?"

"Bobby he's been here six months. He'll be here."

"Okay I guess." Bobby slumped back in his seat.

"We'll go see some more tomorrow." Rob added.

"Oh damn! We can't go. My sister is coming down to visit." I said.

"That's okay. Don't worry about it."

"Yeah but I would really like to go." I said.

Rob dropped us off at home. "Thanks for taking us. It was fun. We'll call you to see how you make out." I said.

"Thanks man." Jack said as he shook Rob's hand.

"Good Luck. Bye Bobby." I said.

"Bye." Bobby said as he gave a wave.

"Later." Rob replied as they drove off.

That night I could not get Beemer out of my mind. I kept thinking about him being in the shelter for so long and how he loved being outside free to run around. I turned to Jack. "Do you think Rob is going back to get Beemer?"

Jack shrugged. "Not sure."

"Well if he doesn't then I am."

Chapter 2 – Adoption

My sister and family came down on Sunday as planned. I was so excited as we were getting to spend time with my sister and her husband and their new son Mikey who they adopted last October. He is so adorable with blonde hair and blue eyes. He has the greatest laugh. We were having so much fun and they stayed much later than expected so we never got a chance to call Rob. Busy with work all week we actually didn't get to call Rob until the following Saturday.

"Call him Jack, call him. I am dying to know if they got another puppy or went back for Beemer."

"I am sure he would have called if he got one."

"You don't know that. Maybe he is busy with the new puppy. C'mon just call him."

"Alright already." Jack dialed Rob but there was no answer.

I was waving my hand and whispered "Leave him a message."

Jack nodded "Hey Rob it's Jack. We… I mean Louann is dying to know if you found a dog. Give us a call when you get a chance."

As Jack hung up I chimed in "Very funny. But it's true." I said with a grin. "Damn. Oh well hopefully he will call back soon."

Rob has three children and Bobby is the youngest. Rob is divorced and Bobby comes to stay with him on the weekends. He thought getting a dog would be good for Bobby when he came to stay and for company for himself too. His other son and daughter were older and busy with college. Bobby was still in high school.

That afternoon the phone rang. "Jack!" I yelled. "It's Rob." I couldn't wait so I answered. "Hi how are you? So did you get a puppy?"

I heard a laugh on the other end. "Well."

"What what I am dying to know!"

"We went to a few other shelters but they really did not have a lot of puppies at this time. They said they would be expecting some soon and we could put our name on a waiting list."

"Oh that's a shame." I was so disappointed. You would think it was me who was getting one. "How long do you have to wait?"

"They couldn't say exactly maybe a few weeks."

Jack walked over and I was shaking my head. "Oh so you are going to wait then? Is Bobby ok with it?"

"Well no. That's why I'm calling. I ended up going back to surprise Bobby and adopted Beemer."

"WHAT? Oh my God that is so great! I knew he was the one. I just knew it! That is terrific! Congratulations!"

"Calm down...Geez I think you are more excited than Bobby." We both laughed.

"Well it is exciting. How is he doing?"

"Hard to tell so far. He is just walking around smelling everything. I wanted to see if you guys wanted to come over for dinner. I am just going to throw some burgers on the grill."

"Yes yes! I would love it. Hold on. Let me just ask Jack." I looked over at Jack as I held my hand over the phone. "They got Beemer, Rob said we should come over – okay?"

"Yeah sure."

I turned back to the phone. "Okay great – how about if we pick up dessert?"

"Sounds good. Come by around 5."

"Yay – see you soon."

"Later."

"I think we should get something for Beemer don't you? Maybe a toy or some treats." I said to Jack.

"Yes we can get something."

We went to one of the Pet Supply stores close by. I was looking at the toys. Jack said "We probably shouldn't get cookies or treats as we don't know what they have to feed him."

"How about a toy?"

"Hmmm again not sure what he can have." Jack headed over to the bed section. They had all kinds of beds and blankets all rolled up. "How about a blanket?"

I walked over to where Jack was. "That may be good. Do you think he bought Beemer a bed?"

"Well if he did or didn't he can still use a blanket."

Beemer's Tale 12

We picked out a red white and blue blanket with stars on it. We then drove to the bakery to get dessert. Of course I picked something chocolate – yum. And then we went right to Rob's house.

Rob lived in a Ranch style house with 2 bedrooms, living room with a fireplace which I absolutely love. The kitchen was in the back of the house and led out to a deck and had a fenced in yard. It was perfect for a dog.

Rob's house was different from our house. Jack and I bought my grandparent's house when we got married. It is a 2 bedroom bungalow type house. It is also a ranch but has a living room, kitchen and porch on the side with the 2 bedrooms and bathroom in the back. We also have a detached garage behind the house.

When we got to the front steps Rob opened the door. "Hello how are you?" I said.

"Good. Good." Rob replied.

I kissed Rob on the cheek. "Here's dessert." and handed him the box.

"Great thanks. C'mon back. Bobby and Beemer are in the yard."

I set my purse and the bag with the blanket down on the couch. We followed Rob out on the deck and saw Bobby and Beemer running around in the grass. "Oh he really is so cute. I think you made a good choice." I said.

I wanted to run over and pet Beemer but did not want to interrupt them. Bobby threw a ball and Beemer ran after it and picked it up.

"Bring it here." Bobby said. Beemer just waited. "Come bring it here." And still Beemer waited. Bobby took a step closer and Beemer went into a play stand bent forward with his tail wagging in the air. Bobby took another step closer and Beemer spun around and started to run. Bobby had to chase him to get the ball back. Leaning on the deck railing we all just smiled and laughed watching the two of them playing in the yard.

After a bit we went to sit down at the picnic table.

"Guess you will have to teach him how to fetch." I said.

"Yeah. For now they are just having fun."

"That is so great. Can't believe how fast Beemer is – amazing."

"Yes – hope he doesn't crash into the fence." Jack said.

Rob yelled down to Bobby "Why don't you guys take a break and come and have something to eat." Rob went inside and came out with two platters that he set down on the picnic table.

Bobby started to walk toward the deck and Beemer whizzed by him and flew up the stairs. There was a bowl of water in the corner and Beemer went right over to get a drink. When he was done I said "Hi Beemer." He came over to where Jack and I were sitting. He was very friendly and wagging his tail. I petted his head and said "Good boy. Did you have fun?"

"Wow this is quite a spread. Thought it was just going to be burgers." Jack said. Rob was really a great cook. Jack likes to cook too. I am lucky because that definitely is not my forte but I do love to eat. Rob made stuffed mushrooms, one of Jack's favorites, that were delicious. Rob also made an Antipasto platter for appetizer. Even Rob's burgers were gourmet with toppings like fresh mozzarella and roasted peppers.

Beemer's Tale 14

We all ate and even Beemer got a little taste of a burger.

"Well you really out did yourself. Thank you so much for dinner it was excellent." I said.

"Glad you liked it." Rob replied.

"How about some dessert?" I asked.

Bobby was the first to say "What's for dessert?"

"Chocolate cake. I'll get it." I said.

I went in to get the cake and a knife. We cut the cake and we all enjoyed dessert with a glass of wine except no wine for Bobby of course. "Chocolate and wine go perfect together." I said.

"I prefer just the wine." Rob added.

It was getting late so we helped bring everything inside and cleaned up. Both Bobby and Beemer were relaxing inside after being worn out from running around before and after dinner. Bobby was on the couch and Beemer was on his bed on the floor at the end of the couch. Rob got him a big square bed with a green removable cover.

"We actually brought him something." I picked up the bag off the couch and handed it to Rob. Beemer sat up alert.

Rob took out the blanket. "Nice. Thanks."

Bobby looked over. "Cool."

"We thought it could be for his bed or wherever you think." Jack said.

Rob layed it out on the floor next to Beemer's bed. "This is yours."

Beemer got up and went right over for a sniff and layed down right on top of it.

"I think he likes it." Jack said.

I smiled. "Aww his first blanky."

"Congratulations and enjoy Beemer." I hugged and kissed Rob. "Thank you so much again for dinner it was delicious."

Jack shook Rob's hand "Yeah thanks man. Everything was great."

I then walked over to where Beemer was laying on his new blanket. I knelt down and kissed him on his head. "Goodnight Beemer." Jack waved "Bye Beemer."

On the drive home I was thinking how funny it was that one of Rob's favorite songs is by the Rolling Stones "Gimme Shelter."

Beemer's Tale 16

Beemer – 6 Months

Chapter 3 – Growing Up

The next time we went to Rob's for dinner, a few weeks later, Beemer greeted us at the door. "Hi Beemer." Jack and I said at the same time. Beemer wagged his tail and we gave him pets and hugs.

"So how is he doing?" Jack asked.

"Good he is just a little skittish." Rob said.

"Oh what do you mean?" I said.

Rob moved a box he had on the end table and dropped it on the floor. Beemer went running to the kitchen to hide. Rob laughed. "Every loud noise or moving boxes and bags he does that."

"Aww poor Beemer. Well he just needs some adjustment time. He was in the shelter for a really long time." I said.

"I guess. Hopefully he will get over it. He's a pretty good dog overall."

"Plus you don't know what he went through. Maybe there was a loud noise that scared him when he got lost or he could have even been hit by a car when he got his broken leg."

Jack asked. "How is Bobby doing?"

"Good they get along great. You will have to see his trick he does with Beemer later."

"Oh what's that?" I asked.

Beemer's Tale 18

"You'll see."

"So what's for dinner?"

"Shrimp Parm."

"Excellent!" That is one of Rob's specialties that everyone asks for. Always Perfect.

This time Jack made stuffed mushrooms for appetizer and I brought my contribution of dessert – Cannoli's, Éclairs and Cream Puffs.

After dinner Beemer and Bobby were playing in the yard.

Rob called down. "Bobby show them that thing you do with Beemer."

"Yeah Okay."

"Wait till you see this." Rob said.

We got up from the table and moved to the railing to get a better view.

Bobby is tall and he lifted his hand above his head with the ball. Beemer was locked on watching Bobby. Bobby said "Get it Beemer."

"He just went straight up in the air!" Jack said amazed.

"Wow! That's so high. I can't believe it!" I said. Beemer jumped up so high to get the ball and then did a spin before landing on the ground. Beemer looked like he was flying in the air like something from a Circus Act or a diver from the Olympics.

Rob laughed. "That's a puppy for ya."

"He loves it." Bobby said smiling.

"Yeah. I'll bet." Jack said.

I turned to Rob. "That really is something."

After dinner Rob lit a fire in the fireplace. Rob loved making a big fire. We were enjoying wine as a nite cap. Bobby was playing video games in his room. It was so warm and cozy. I got to sit next to Beemer who was lying on the end of the couch closest to the fire and Jack was on my other side. Rob was in his chair. I felt so happy just watching the fire and petting Beemer.

We got up to leave and Beemer jumped off the couch and retreated to his bed. When we were at the door I said "You know you can bring Beemer to our house any time. We don't have a fenced in yard but he is welcome."

"Ok thanks."

As we said our goodbyes, I took a last look at Beemer. He was snoozing out on his blanket amongst the stars and stripes.

<u>The Deli</u>

>Rob owned a deli located near the high school. On good days he would bring Beemer and leave him outside in the back. He would feed Beemer anything and everything. Garlic, eggs, and all the leftovers from the Deli in addition to his dog food.

>When the high school students came to the deli they spotted Beemer in the back. They immediately went over to pet him. They went inside and one of the boys

asked Rob about him. "Mr. R. Is that your dog back there?"

"Yeah."

"What's his name?" one of the girls asked.

"Beemer."

"He's beautiful." Another girl said. "Yeah he is a really cute doggie." Her friends agreed.

Every day that Beemer was at the Deli the students would take turns or even argue over who got to sit next to him. They would play with him, hug and kiss him. All the kids loved him.

"Hey Mr. R. Can we take him home for a visit?" one boy asked.

Another boy said "Yeah he would love my dog Jakey. He is a Rottweiler."

"I don't think so. No." Rob answered. Rob constantly got requests from the students to mind Beemer, take him for a walk or bring him home.

I myself kept finding extra reasons to go to Rob's to see Beemer. Don't get me wrong not that I didn't love seeing Rob and Bobby too, but Beemer was so damn cute.

Every Saturday Jack and I would go to the Deli for Breakfast or Lunch.

"So have you taught him any tricks? I asked Rob.

He laughed. "Nah no time. Didn't have a chance and Bobby is happy just to run around and play with him. Ever since Bear passed it's good for him to have Beemer." Bear, a shepherd mix, was their childhood dog.

I thought maybe I could try to teach Beemer a trick. I started with giving Paw. So with some of my breakfast in hand I went over and worked with Beemer on giving paw. He was smart. Beemer caught on real quick and even offered his paw without prompting. "Guess he liked the ham." I said. When he gave paw I noticed some of his nails were white and some were black. He also had a little white spot on the back of his neck above his collar.

The next trick we worked on was "Sitting up." I would ask Beemer to sit and then lift his two front Paws and said "Up". It took us quite a number of tries for that one. He would either give paw or try to sit up briefly. It definitely took longer than giving paw. Maybe he was holding out for treats. Eventually he did it and he looked so cute. "Aww Good Boy Beemer. Good Boy!"

As the months went by Beemer was growing up. He got taller and put on some weight.

Several times Rob would stop by with Beemer in 'The Beast'. Beemer had his head out the window with his "Flying Nun" ears blowing the wind. He looked so happy as if he was really flying.

One time Rob stopped over we were standing on the front lawn watching as Beemer was walking around sniffing and peeing on the big oak trees we had.

Beemer's Tale 22

"This week I was ready to kill him."

"Why? What happened?" Jack asked.

"I told you guys I was having the Insurance Man come over to come assess the house for Homeowner's Right?"

"Yes I remember." Jack said.

"Well I didn't bring Beemer to the Deli that day as it was raining. I figured he would be good since I was closing early to meet the Insurance Man at the house."

"I pulled up and the Insurance Guy was already there. So he followed me in and there was Beemer standing on the couch which he totally chewed up! There was foam from the cushions everywhere. I looked at him and said 'What did you do?' Well he immediately jumped off with his head down. I pointed and said I'll deal with you later."

Jack and I could not help but laugh. "That's awful but hilarious! Oh I am so sorry but I can just imagine it." I said.

"Believe me it wasn't funny at the time."

"I'll bet." Jack added.

"So then what happened?" I asked trying to contain my laughter.

"I told the Insurance Guy to have a seat – in my chair of course since the couch was not an option. I let Beemer out in the yard. It worked out ok but I couldn't believe it. He never did anything like that before. Dammit of all days."

"I guess he missed going to the Deli." Jack said.

"Yeah smart ass."

"You know we can watch him anytime if there is something you need to do. Right Jack?" I said.

"Definitely." Jack agreed.

"Ok Thanks. I will keep that in mind."

Beemer's Tale 24

Beemer in the 'Beast'

Beemer 'Growing Up' - Standing Tall

Chapter 4 – Welcome Home

The landlord of Rob's Deli wanted to sell the property unfortunately so Rob had to close the Deli and find a new job. Such a shame as he really had a great business at that location. One day Rob came over with Beemer. "I got a new job."

"You did? That is terrific! Where?" I said.

"I'll be cooking for a Seafood Restaurant."

"That's great. Right up your alley." Jack added. "Congratulations man."

"It's 20 minutes away and I will be gone for a long time and late nights. I was thinking." Rob started rubbing his chin. "It's really not fair to leave Beemer home alone for so long. I can't take him with me and with Bobby only there on weekends …I am thinking of putting a sign up on the grocery bulletin board for someone to adopt Beemer."

"What?" I exclaimed. "You can't do that!" I was stunned. I looked at Jack and then back to Rob.

"Well who's gonna let him out and I can't have him eat another couch!"

"You can't do that. You can't! You don't know who would call. It could be some crazy person!"

"Yeah man. You can't trust what people might do. Would be better to bring him back to the shelter." Jack said.

Without even thinking to check with Jack first I said "No. NO! Absolutely not. We will take him."

Later after Rob left I said to Jack "Sorry, I had to say it. I can't even think of Beemer going back to the shelter after spending six months there or worse going to some person not even screened from the grocery store! I can't."

"Yes that would be bad." Jack agreed.

"I just can't let that happen. I love him." And there it was – I wanted Beemer more than anything. I really loved him. I had a lot of family dogs in my life but none were like Beemer to me and he would be the first one ever that was mine.

We did talk to Rob to make sure Bobby was ok with giving Beemer away. "Are you sure? How does Bobby feel about it?"

"Okay. He understands. The Ex got a new dog. It's a little white fluffy thing. Bobby is going to college next year anyway so he is good with it."

"Well you know Bobby is welcome to come by anytime to visit Beemer and see him." I said sincerely.

"I'll tell him."

<u>The Day Has Arrived</u>

> I remember that day in November 2002. It was November 16 to be exact. I was so excited. Beemer was coming to live with us!
>
> Rob pulled up with Beemer hanging out the window. It was his last ride flying in 'The Beast'. He got out and opened the passenger door to let Beemer out. He jumped down and ran over.

"Hey Beemer." I bent down to pet him.

"Beem." Jack called and Beemer trotted over.

"Here you go." Rob held out a big garbage bag with all his belongings. Rob packed up his food, bed, leash, bowl and even brought the blanket we gave him.

"Thank you. He will definitely be well taken care of. Please tell Bobby he is always welcome and of course you too. We can even bring Beemer over if that is better."

"Yeah. I think he would like that." Rob was definitely a little sad to give Beemer up.

"Always. Anytime." Jack said.

Rob patted Beemer on his side. "Be good Beem." And off he went. Beemer just watched and realizing he wasn't going in "The Beast" he then turned and ran toward the back yard. Beemer's new back yard.

"Welcome Home Beemer!" I said smiling as I ran after him.

Beemer's Tale 28

Beemer Arrived!

Ready to Play in his New Backyard!

Chapter 5 – Daily Life – Part 1

Technically Beemer was rescued twice. Once with Rob and then with us. Beemer adapted so well right away. It didn't seem to bother him being in a new place and with different people, but he did already know us. Maybe because he was still young, but we were so glad he seemed happy.

We introduced Beemer to the neighborhood. Our next door neighbor and friend Sam was the first to meet Beemer. Sam and Beemer hit it off right away. "He is a good looking dog. He is tall and muscular and dam he can run." Sam said. Sam was a construction worker so appreciated anyone in good shape. Sam patted him on the back and enjoyed watching him run across his lawn, which was a double lot, and then all the way back to ours. Sam had a Lhasa Apso who was much older than Beemer named Gizmo. Beemer and Gizzy, which we called her for short, instantly became friends. Beemer was so gentle with her considering she was so much smaller than him. We laughed and said "Beemer has a girlfriend."

We quickly fell into a routine with Beemer. During the week I would go to work and Jack was home most of the time with Beemer as Jack was working freelance.

Jack and I unfortunately did not have children of our own, but we had many nieces, nephews and our friend's children to love and spoil. We had spent several years taking care of aging parents and their pets before Beemer. So now Beemer is like our kid. He is our day to day focus.

Beemer's Tale 30

"Do you think we should let him on the furniture?" I asked Jack. "You know once you let them on then there is no going back." Jack shrugged.

"Okay so maybe the couch but we will put his dog bed in our bedroom and he can sleep on that at night." We learned how really sweet Beemer is while living with him. He loves to hang out with us on the couch. He would always sit next to one of us or even try to sit in our lap. "Beem you are not exactly Gizzy's size." Jack would say. But we didn't mind. It is fun.

Our house is small but we make it work. We have a large sectional couch for maximum seating in front of the windows. The couch has two recliner sections and a console in the middle. Beemer would stand up straight with his two front feet on the console looking out the window. When we would look over or come out of the bedroom and see him standing there he looked like "Rin Tin Tin." Rin-Tin-Tin, a German Shepherd, was rescued from a World War I battlefield by an American Soldier and went on to be a film and TV star. "Hey there's 'Rin Tin Tinny.' Jack would say.

Beemer in 'Rin Tin Tin' Pose

In front of the couch we have a long coffee table. It is actually a lobster trap converted with a glass top. It was very cool and fit perfectly for a shore house. Beemer maneuvered around the coffee table with no problem but we thought it may be a good idea to give him a little more room for jumping on and off the couch. We swapped out our Lobster table for a smaller one. We stored the Lobster table in the basement as I could not part with it. I thought we may be able to use it in the future if we moved to a larger house. We had a small square coffee table my Mom had given us so we swapped it out and it was perfect.

We thought Beemer looked adorable in every pose. Whenever Beemer would do a 'beg' or 'sit up' position like a Bunny Rabbit, people always gave an "Awww" when he did that trick.

Beemer's Tale 32

Beemer looked so cute when he was cold and curled up in a ball on the bed or the couch. I just wanted to scoop him up and put him on my lap. Beemer didn't seem to like to be picked up. If we tried he would get all squirmy so we would just call him over instead and he would jump up on the couch. Then I would snuggle close to him and gave him hugs and kisses.

Spy vs. Spy in Mad Magazine

Sometimes when Beemer was laying down he would point his head down so only his nose was touching the couch or he would be sitting and point his nose toward his chest. He looked just like Spy vs. Spy from Mad Magazine. So funny.

Bedtime

At bedtime Beemer always came with us and would lay on his bed in the bedroom. One morning I got up to go to the bathroom. When I came out I saw Beemer on the bed with Jack hugging him.

"Oh no." I said and laughed. They looked so adorable. "Well you know it's all over now don't you?"

They just looked at me and Jack smiled.

And so after that we had a total Beemer fixture on our bed. "It's time for bed Beem" I would say and most of time he would hop off the couch and follow us to bed. Sometimes Beemer would go to bed ahead of us. We have a full bed and Beemer loved to lay across the bed and not the long way. When it was time to sleep if he went in earlier than us we had to turn him so we could fit. We gently moved him and sometimes he would give a "Hmmph" sound, never a growl but just a noise letting us know "Hey – I am comfortable. Go find your own bed." That always made us laugh. "Sorry Beem we need to get in too." We were like a reverse Oreo - the three of us trying to fit and sleep on the bed. Sometimes we did wish we had room for a bigger bed.

Beemer's Tale 34

Beemer in Bed

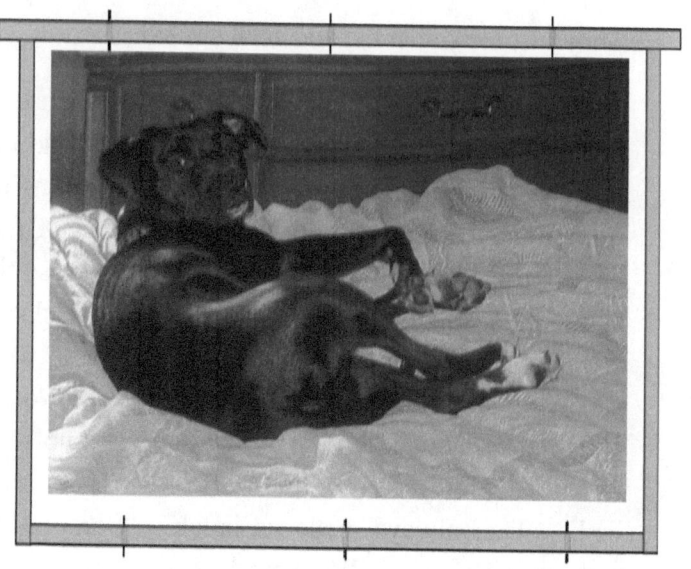

We noticed Beemer never liked to be in a room with the door closed. If you shut him in he would just stand at the door and not relax. We never closed the door to our bedroom. We wondered if it brought back memories from his shelter days.

Morning

Beemer looked so sweet in the morning when he just opened his eyes and would do a stretch. He would put his front leg in the air and we said it was his "John Travolta" in Saturday Night Fever pose. Then Beemer would show his tummy for a rub. I would sing "Stayin Alive Stayin Alive ooh ooh ooh." Beemer would wag his tail and it would make a "Thump Thump" sound on the bed. We loved that. Sometimes he would stretch with his two front legs out. "It's Superman." He looked like he was flying. So many laughs that we looked forward to waking up.

When I would get out of bed in the morning on work days I would whisper "Sleep for me my beauty." And kiss him on his head.

Some mornings I would get up early before work to exercise. I would do my tape of Denise Austin. I loved her as she mixed both Yoga, Stretching with Cardio. Beemer usually stayed in bed with Jack but on some occasions he would come out to see me while I was exercising. The very first time he did this he followed what I was doing. We did Downward Facing Dog together as we both stretched. "Beem you are doing it. Good Boy." He then earned the name "Yoga Boy." Every time he came out to exercise with me I would say "Good Morning Yoga Boy." He would come and stretch and sometimes want to go out after or sometimes go back to bed.

After a shower and getting dressed if Beemer did not come out for Yoga then sometimes Beemer would get up to go out. After going out he would jump on the couch or sometimes he would go back to bed with Jack. Either way before I left for work I would say "Have a great day my boy. I love you!" I would blow him a kiss. "I'll see you later."

Beemer's 'Saturday Night Fever' Pose

When I came home from work I was so happy to see Beemer I would race inside to see him. "Beem!" I would walk in put my stuff down and open my arms for him to run over for a hug. Or if he was outside I would drop my bag and he would come running to see me. Such a joy to be greeted with such excitement and tail wagging.

<u>Fence</u>

Our house is set up with two front doors and not a back door. One opened to the living room and the other to the porch on the other end of the house. Funny we called this our back door. Jack had set up one of those stakes in the ground in the backyard that would swivel as the leash would go around. He set up a long lead to run from the stake to the front door on the porch so we could hook Beemer up and not always have to take him out on a leash. For the most part that worked great except that we had a large oak tree in the back yard and sometimes Beemer would get hooked around it with the lead and we had to go get him.

"I think we really need to get a fence." I said to Jack. "It would be a lot easier to let Beemer out. What do you think?"

"Yes but how are we going to do that without a back door?"

"Well it would cost a lot more to switch the door from the front to the back of the house but maybe we could have the fence come around to be only in front of the side front door." I drew a picture of my idea. "This is what I was thinking."

Jack studied my rough drawing. "That may work but we will have to get an estimate." "Definitely – who do you think we should call?"

"From what I know the people at work recommend this one place south of here, they all say they are one of the best."

"Okay let's call them."

We called, got an estimate and set it up. They came on a freezing day in January. We could not even imagine how they could dig a hole in the ground as it was so frozen. Jack offered them something to drink and they wanted a coke. They opened the soda, took a drink and set it down. Shortly after that the soda started to foam and come up out of the can as it was getting frozen.

"Omg how can they work when even the soda is getting frozen!" I said.

"I guess that's why they are the experts."

Somehow they managed and the fence came out beautiful. We picked an aluminum fence, so no maintenance, about 4 foot high with vertical bars that you could see though so Beemer would have a view. No more lead and getting caught around the tree. The first time letting Beemer out without the lead was great. He waited as we always had to hook him up.

"It's okay Beem, go run." Jack said. And he did. We went out after him. Beemer loved the freedom with the fence.

Beemer Smiling Behind His New Fence

The fence was set up so we had a gate in the front of the house and another gate in the back. We had a detached garage behind our house and a long stone covered driveway. Beemer would spend most of his time sitting out front watching and observing everything that was going on. We put one of those padded mats down so it would be more comfortable for him. Whenever he saw people visiting Sam's he got excited and thought we would let him out to run and visit with Sam and Gizzy. "Not today Beem."

If it was nice and we were working in the yard planting or working on the lawn we would have him out with us to enjoy the day. Every time we opened the back gate, even if we did it so quietly he would hear the little click and run from the front to the back.

"OMG he hears it every time!" I said to Jack.

"He thinks something is going on."

Sometimes we would let him out and he could walk and sniff the stones and other times we said "Wait here Beem. Nothing is going on. We will take you to the park in a little bit." We talked to him like he understood. We think most of the time he did.

We noticed Beemer loved to be chased. If you threw him a ball he would go in his play pose and wanted you to chase him just like he did with Bobby. It was so fun running around the big oak tree in the middle of our yard. Beemer had this thing we called "The Spin" where if you were chasing him and getting too close he would spin around in a circle and take off in a different direction.

"Did you see that?" I called to Jack.

"Yes. I can't believe he is going so fast."

We had chase fests around the big oak tree. I would peek around one side of the tree and Beemer would see me and get in his play pose – downward facing dog like in Yoga. Then I would peek around the other side of the tree. Beemer would hop and go down in his play pose again. I would do it a third time and he was ready. I started to run around to catch him and he took off. We would run in circles around the tree. When he finally had enough he would retreat to his 'Den' as we called it. He would go under the bush against the fence where there was a patch of dirt underneath. When it got hot outside he would go there as it was cool there since it is shaded. Beemer would dig up the dirt a little and lay down.

We noticed that Beemer never barked. When he was excited to see people or other dogs he would let out a little whine noise which was so cute, but never a bark. Most of the neighbors behind us never even knew we had a dog.

"Do you think he can bark?" I asked Jack.

"I don't know."

"We'll have to ask Rob if he ever barked when he lived with him."

Beemer in his 'Den'

Beemer in the Front Yard

Beemer in the Back Yard

Beemer Hangin Out in the Driveway

Work from Home

We had a desk set up in the spare bedroom where we kept our computer. Whenever I worked from home I would work there. Beemer would come every so often to check in and say hello.

"Hi Beem. You coming to help me good boy?" And I would give him a pet and a hug.

Beemer was never a fan of jumping on the bed in the spare bedroom. It was set against the wall and for some reason he did not like it. Only time he jumped up there was if others were staying over. Then in the morning he would jump up to greet them or tell them it was time to get up. "Well Good morning Beemer." Jack's brother would say when he stayed over. Also one of our musician friends Lenny, who came down to visit often, would close the door if he wanted to sleep late otherwise Beemer would have definitely went in early.

Shopping

We thought it would be great to take Beemer to Pet Smart as it was a store he was actually welcome to come inside with us. We took Beemer to let him pick some new toys. It was so fun going down the toy aisle. Beemer would sniff the toys but never take one. "It's okay Beemer. Pick one. Anyone you like." He finally went over and gently picked a little stuffed ball. "That's it my boy. You like that one? It's yours."

While there we saw this really cool collar. It was black with colorful X's on it red, blue, yellow and orange.

"I think this would look great on Beemer." Jack said.

"Me too. Let's get it."

The one he had now was solid red which was great, but when we got home and put the new one on it was a perfect fit. It showed up great on him. We got many compliments and people always asked us where we got his collar.

We also took Beemer there to get his nails cut and then we would let him pick out a new toy afterwards. He is so good. Some of the dogs would have an accident or pee in the aisle. "No Pee here Beem." And he never did even though we were sure he could smell that others did. I thought I could do his nails. I even bought one of those safe nail cutters but I caved and chickened out. I never wanted to hurt him in case I didn't do it right.

Best to let someone more experienced to do it. When he was done we would go in the toy aisle. We would hold up different toys we thought he would like. Some he would just smell but when he went to take one we knew that was the one. We would buy him a little bag of treats too for the way home. "Beem you went shopping."

He was happy when he saw other dogs there as we went down the aisles.

Toys and Bones

Beemer loves to get new toys. He liked the stuffed animal ones with a squeaker. Whenever we gave him one he would run with delight into the living room. He would parade around with it wagging his tail as if it was a prized possession. Beemer would then lay down on the rug and chew and chew until he got tired or the squeaker got a hole in it and would not squeak anymore. He kept it with him on the couch for awhile and then he was pretty much done with it so the toy went to the retired pile.

Sometimes we would play hide the toy to make it last longer before giving it to him. If you put it under your arm he would bring his head there trying to burrow in to get it and it soon became a ticklefest.

We keep a basket on the floor with all of Beemer's toys. Sometimes he would go to the pile and fish an old one out and give a chew. Whenever we had friends and family over and if they brought their dogs for a visit all the dogs would have a field day going to the toy basket. They would get one to chew for awhile and then go get another one. There would be toys all over the floor when they left.

Beemer also loves rawhides and bones. If we gave him a rawhide he would chew and chew until he finished it or it was a gloppy mess and then we would take it away. We were amazed that he always let us take it and just looked. He never growled or was aggressive in any way. Eventually we gave him smaller ones so it was not so intense or long to finish.

One day in the pet store we found the real bones with a little meat on it and started to give him those as a special treat. Those are his new favorite. We always monitored so that once the meat was gone we took it away.

Beemer with All His Toys and Bones

Beemer's Tale 48

<u>Photo Op</u>

One day I saw in the paper they were having a "Pet Photo" booth at the Wal-Mart near our house. "I want to take him to get his picture taken."

Jack looked at me like I was crazy. "What?"

"He is so cute. We should have a professional picture taken." Beemer is funny about that. Whenever we tried to take his picture he would always put his ears back. "Beemer. Look here." I would say. We would whistle and make noises to try to make his ears perk up. It was very hard to get a perfect picture. I called and made an appointment. I remember driving up to the sign in the parking lot which was next to a trailer. "Oh boy this is going to be fun." I said to Jack.

Beemer had so much energy. We walked up the ramp and walked into the trailer. There was a bale of hay against the wall with a fake window as the background. It had artificial butterflies around the window. The photographer said "Do you think you can get him up there."

"Sure no problem." I said. He jumped up on the couch and bed fairly easily so I thought he would have no problem. I patted the bail of hay. "Up up Beemer." At first Beemer backed away not sure what it he was supposed to do.

"Maybe you could pick him up." The photographer said.

"Mmmm I'm not sure he would like that. Let me try again." I said "C'mon Beemer up up!" and patted the top of the hay bail. Beemer jumped so fast he almost knocked the whole thing over. "Whoa. Okay Beem." I grabbed Beemer's collar to steady him. "Sit and stay." I said as I held my hand out. And he did. It took quite a few tries with the photographer to get Beemer to look without his ears back but finally there was a photo op.

It turned out to be a beautiful picture of Beemer. We hung it on the wall over the couch.

Beemer's Portrait

Beemer's Tale 50

Travels and Car Rides

Beemer loves car rides and we took him everywhere. I called him my 'Wingman' as he went on all errands. Even if Jack did not go Beemer always came along for the ride.

Saturdays were errand day and play day. I was always so happy to be home and get to spend the day with my Beem. I would wake up and sing to Beem "It's Saturday, Saturday, Saturday, Saturday!" to the tune of Elton John's "Saturday Night's Alright."

We would get up, go outside to do business, have breakfast and then head out.

I would even tell him where we were going. I gave him the plan of the day. He really seemed to understand words and most of what I was saying. "Come on Beem, we are going to see Frank at the Bank, do errands and then come home for 'Lunch'." Frank was the VP of our local bank. Beemer always got a cookie there. The teller would see him sitting in the backseat and say "Oh he is so cute. Would he like a cookie?"

"Yes he loves withdrawals." I replied.

After the bank if I had to get or return books I would say we are going to the *"Library Beem."* I would say it like Clarence from 'It's a Wonderful Life'. There was a little park area behind the parking lot so after going to the Library we would let him out of the car to run around.

Then we would go to the cleaners or any other errands needed.

After errands we would go home for a little rest and after lunch it was play time. "Ready Beem? We are going to the park." He would fly off the couch with tail wagging. Beemer went straight for the door.

We had linoleum in the kitchen so sometimes he would go so fast that he lost traction and would slide a bit heading to the back door. That is how we usually went out to go in the fenced in back yard, but when we were going to the car we would go out the front door from the living room. We would have to call him back and say "No no – we are going out this way and he would turn around again sliding to get to the door. We decided to get runner rugs to put in the kitchen to help him from sliding. When his nails got a little long it was funny as he walked in the kitchen it sounded like he was tap dancing across the floor. "Doot doot doot." We would say "There he goes." Then it was time to get his nails cut.

When we went to the grocery store sometimes we would bring him. "We will be back in a little bit Beem." We would say when we got out of the car. While waiting in the car we always said he was 'Stealth.' Often no one even knew he was there as he would lay down. He never jumped up and barked at anyone who walked by. Often as we were coming out of the store and walking to the car we could see he was sitting up and looking out to see if were coming back. People would be looking at him smiling and talking to him. As we came over they would tell us "Wow he is so well behaved. We didn't even know he was there." "He is such a good looking dog." "What is his name?" "What kind of dog is he?" I cannot even count how many times we get that question.

Sometimes people would laugh as we always had a remote starter in the car so if it was cold we would leave the heat on or if it was warm we would put on the air conditioning as needed. We were very cautious especially in the summer. We would either go early or often waited till the end of day when the sun was less hot to take him.

Some places we did not take him as we did not want to leave him in the car in the parking lot. We were worried someone may steal him. He was so friendly and probably would go with anyone for a car ride.

We even brought Beemer to Rob's house a number of times after Beemer came to live with us. Beemer remembered his first house. After greeting Rob, Beemer always made a mad dash to the back door to go out in the yard.

Vet

We decided to keep going to the Vet where Rob had taken him. It was close by. The Doctors were a husband and wife team with two other Doctors, Techs and Staff. Beemer's Doctor was Dr. M. He was terrific. Dr. M. was so patient and explained everything to you. If Dr. M. wasn't available then Beemer would see his wife Dr. H who was also terrific. Everyone there was so wonderful, caring and supportive. Beemer never minded going for his annual check-up. So many dogs get so afraid or nervous. Beemer was very comfortable there and for him the bonus was he got to see other dogs and cats.

SummerFest

Every summer on the first weekend in June the town would close part of the street down in front of the park down the street from our house. They had food vendors, crafters and activities for kids. Jack and I would go earlier in the day and look at all the vendors and then later in the day we would bring Beemer back and get something to eat. There were less people at the end of the day so Beemer would not get stepped on and it was not as hot in the sun. We saw many of our friends and neighbors at the festival so it was always a fun time.

We always went to one of the vendors with fresh seafood; Clams, Shrimp, Oysters and Fish of the Day. One of Beemer's favorites is Tuna Bites. Jack would have clams and Beemer and I would share the Tuna Bites.

One year we saw our old neighbors who moved away. They sold their house to get a bigger house to have more room for their children and dogs. They had two children and one on the way and two American Bulldogs. Mick and Jancy. When they lived next door Mick and Beemer were friends and liked to run around on the front lawn. They got Jancy right before they moved and she was a little shy.

"Hey guys how are you doing? How's the new place?"

"Good Good. So much more room."

"Yes I bet. Definitely more than the old place." Jack said.

"Where are the kids?"

"They are with their Grandparent's so Pete and I get a little break."

"Nice. Bet they are growing like weeds."

"Yes definitely too fast ."

"Beemer's looking good." Pete said as he pet Beemer.

"Yes he is doing great. How's Mick and Jancy?"

"Good. They are loving the new backyard."

"So good to see you guys."

"Same here. You'll have to come by sometime to see the new house."

"That would be great. Thanks."

We said our goodbyes and then Beemer and I finished our Tuna Bites.

On our walk back home from the Summerfest this one time there was a man in a truck waiting for the light to change. He rolled down the window and said "That's a good looking dog. I had one once that looked like him." "Awesome. Thank You. He's a good guy and is a Rescue from the Shelter." "That is so great." The light changed and he had to go. He waved and said "Take good care of him. Have a good day." "You too!" I looked at Jack and said "That was so nice. And taking care of Beemer - Yes we will, always."

<u>Vacation</u>

It was great if Jack and I wanted to get away Rob would come and stay at our house to take care of Beemer. Our friend Sam would let Beemer out when he got home from work since he got home around 3:30P and then Beemer would be good until Rob got off work. Having been in the shelter for so long I could never put Beemer in a kennel. I never wanted him to think he was being sent back there. We thought it was so much better for him to be in his own home and have someone mind him there. It was perfect that it was Rob which Beemer knew so well.

When I mentioned to a friend of mine we were going away for the weekend she said "Just send him to a kennel. He'll love it. Our dog loves being there when we are gone."

"No you don't understand. I NEVER want to send him to a kennel. Your dog did not live in a shelter for six months!"

There is nothing wrong with going to a kennel there are many wonderful places, but we never wanted to put him in a kennel so Beemer would not think he was back at the shelter or we were giving him away. We just did not think it was right for him. We wanted him to have the comfort of his own home and/or be with people he knew.

Beemer's Tale 56

Beemer Comfy on his Couch *and*
*****Fast Asleep on the Bed*****

What's in a Name

We always thought that Beemer's name fit him perfectly. One of a kind and very unique just like him. Jack said "Kudos to whoever named him."

"I totally agree." I said. It could not be a better fit.

Our joke is as we tell everyone "At least we have a Beemer." He was shiny and jet black with white wall tires and very fast. Although to us Beemer is more precious than any car could ever be. We were not sure whoever named him at the shelter, but we thank them as they got it right. It is something that everyone wants and so is he. We did often wonder if it was maybe because he was hit by a car when he got his broken leg, or for some other reason but we will never know.

We also thought about how Beemer ended up on the side of the road. "Beem what happened to you?" We wished he could tell us. "Did you try to cross the street and got hit by a car?" I hate to think that someone actually tried to hurt him in any way or left him there. Every time I hear of any kind of abuse cases I get so angry. "How could anyone do such a thing?" I will never understand. I don't have high blood pressure but think my blood pressure goes off the charts just hearing or thinking about it!

Some people did not get his name right when we told them. Many people called him "Boomer."

Over time we had many nicknames for Beemer.

> 'Beem' for short was the most popular.

> Beemer loved to be in the sun. He looked so handsome with the sun shining on him. He is our "Sun Beem."

> That's my 'B".

Beemy or Beemykins.

Beemy Weemy.

'The Beemster'.

'Beemer my Beemer.' I would say quoting the Walt Whitman poem 'Captain my Captain'.

"Best Boy in the World."

"Handsomest Guy in Town."

Every day at some point I would whisper in his ear or tell him "Beemer you are the 'Best Boy in the World' and the 'Handsomest Guy in Town.'"

"There's my handsome boy." When he would come over.

"How you doing 'B'?"

"Hey you cutie patootie." When he was just sitting on the couch.

"Hugs for my Love Bug." Whenever I would hug him.

"My Seabiscut." If we gave him a bath after drying him we would drape the towel over his back. Beemer looked like a winning racehorse. You are always a winner in our book.

"My Wingman" as you came with me everywhere.

I call you 'My Selkie' – just waiting for you to come out.

I call you my 'Seelie' – you were like a good fairy helping others.

"My Beauty" – as you are my Black Beauty like in the movie.

Whatever name we called you – you always answered and knew it was out of love.

Beemer with a Wink

Chapter 6 – Training

"You know Beemer still really pulls on our walks. He is so strong and always wants to run. I think maybe we should take him to training." I said to Jack.

"That may be a good idea." Jack replied.

Beemer was also still a little timid and shy of big boxes or when we brought in bags from the grocery store just like when he lived with Rob. We thought training would help him on walks in addition to building his confidence.

Back then Cesar Milan, who we love, was not yet on TV to give guidance so we looked for a place or school close by for Obedience Training. We searched in the paper and online. "This one looks pretty good and has a great rating. They have all kinds of training." I said to Jack.

Jack looked at the website. "Sure let's check it out."

<u>Obedience Training</u>

>When I called they said their Basic Obedience Session was already in progress but they invited us to come and observe some classes. The first time we went we set it up to meet with the instructors before class started. It was only about 20 minutes from our house. Since I worked full time during the week we went on Saturday. The place was huge. There was a training building in front and behind it was a big open field where there was all kinds of equipment set up. I had read online they

offer Agility classes where the dogs are taught to go through a course of obstacles and equipment for fun or competition. We arrived a little early to let Beemer sniff around before meeting with the instructors. Of course Beemer watered a few trees. As we headed toward the building out came a woman with dark curly hair and a big smile. "Hi I am Mary."

"Hi I am Louann and this is my husband Jack. And this is Beemer." As I waved my hand toward Beemer.

Mary leaned forward immediately to pet Beemer. "Hello Beemer." Beemer came closer and was wagging his tail.

"Paul leads all the obedience classes." Mary explained. "Myself or one of our other staff members help out. We also offer Agility Classes as you asked about on the phone but Obedience is a Prerequisite. We can see how he does and then you can decide."

"Well he loves to run." Jack added.

"Well then he might definitely like Agility." Come inside and you can sit on the side and watch the next class.

"Great. Thank you." We followed Mary inside and saw there were folding chairs along the wall. We went and sat down. Beemer was so excited seeing all the other dogs. He thought it was play time. We tried to make him sit still. Every time a dog got close he would stand up and try to get close to sniff or try to play.

We observed that at the beginning of class Paul would give an overview of what they were going to do that day and then everyone would go through practice exercises. At the end of class you would get an instruction sheet with homework that you had to practice during the week before the next class.

We definitely saw progress in the dogs by the end of the class. We signed up for their next session.

In April 2003, we started our 8 week course for Basic Obedience. On our first day we walked in and waited against the wall.

There were so many different kinds of dogs in our class; a husky, a poodle, a boxer, a golden retriever, a westie, a cattle dog, a doberman and others in addition to Beemer. Beemer wanted to play with them all. There were about 15 in total. We noticed Beemer was very unique to his class; the only Lab or Pit Mix in the group.

We learned the commands to sit, stay, stand, down and heel. Each time you would give a command once and if they did not do it you would put them in that position and then repeat "Good sit" or whatever the command was.

When it was time to go to school I would look at Beemer on the couch and say "Time for School Beemer. Ready?" Beemer would jump off the couch and go to the door. "Good ready!"

At our third session Beemer was still pulling on the leash. I was very gentle with my instructions to him as I did not want to be harsh since Beemer is so sweet. Paul came over. "You need to take control." Paul showed me the proper way to correct Beemer when he was pulling. I felt bad but he was right. I still didn't want to do it but realized it was for Beemer's benefit.

"Easy Beemer. Easy. Good heel. Good heel." Paul always came over to correct the class members as needed. Beemer would often get distracted as he loved seeing the other dogs. When he had to sit or lay down he would give out a little whine as he wanted off the leash to run around with them. "Shhh Beem." I would say. Everyone nearby turned to look and laughed when they heard him.

After class we would take Beemer to the park to play. We thought maybe we should take him to the park first before class to wear him out and then maybe he would be less excited. We decided it was best to let him learn in class and save the park for a reward.

We consistently did our homework all week every week and by the end of our 8 weeks, Beemer graduated with flying colors. Consistency is definitely the key. You can't do it one day and not the next. You have to practice and not just do it while in class, but it is totally worth the investment of time. Beemer no longer pulled on the leash and listened to commands. He still did give his little whine when excited to see the other dogs but that was okay.

Mary came over after the last class. "Congratulations Beemer." And she have him a big pet. "Beemer has done so well."

"Yes we are so happy and proud of him."

"We have an Intermediate Session in Obedience that you may want to consider. I think it would be good for him if you are still thinking of Agility."

"Yes we would definitely like to do Agility with him."

"They have a Canine Good Citizen test at the end of the Intermediate Session. Beemer has such a sweet personality and in case you want to think about the Pet Therapy Training."

"Great thank you. Yes that may be good since we take him to see my Mom in an Assisted Living Facility. We will definitely think about it. When does the Intermediate Class start?"

"Next week."

I looked at Jack and he nodded. "Perfect. We would like to sign up."

Beemer "Good Sit"

Intermediate Obedience

When we arrived for our first Intermediate Session we went inside and waited against the wall like last time. In walked a lady with a dalmation who was so adorable. I always think of "101 Dalmations" when I see a dalmation – I love that movie. Beemer tried to go right over to see them.

"Hi this is Beemer."

The lady laughed. "He is so cute. This is Misty and I am Katie."

"Nice to meet you. I am Louann and this is my husband Jack."

We made introductions as Beemer and Misty were circling around each other and sniffing to get acquainted. Tails were wagging so I think Beemer made his first school friend.

"So you are here for the Intermediate Training?" I asked.

"Yes I want to train Misty to be a Therapy Dog."

"Oh that is terrific. Such a good cause. We bring Beemer to see my Mom and everyone always wants to pet him when we walk in."

"How about you with Beemer?"

"For now we are just trying to get him to continue to listen and walk well on the leash." Jack said.

Katie laughed. "Yes that is our goal too."

"We may consider Agility as Beemer has lots of energy or maybe even do the Pet Therapy also. Mary thought he would be a good candidate." I added.

"Yes he seems so sweet. I think so too. Misty and Beemer could do it together." Katie replied.

"That would be great."

As the weeks progressed Beemer and Misty always greeted each other first thing before class. They both did very well in addition to the rest of the class. After our 7 weeks both Misty and Beemer Graduated and were Officially Good Canine Citizens. You received a Canine Good Citizen Certificate.

Mary came over to congratulate us. Beemer went right over to see Mary wagging his tail. He loves Mary. Mary said "Beemer you have really done so well. So much better than your first day."

We laughed. "Yes we can't believe it. It has really made such a difference. All thanks to all of you in training."

Mary smiled. "Well you did the work too. Have you thought about considering Pet Therapy? I think Beemer would do really well."

"Thanks yes I think we are definitely considering it."

"You have met Cole during the Obedience Training. He does all the Pet Therapy Training."

"Oh yes Cole is great. He has given many helpful suggestions."

"You can talk to him also if you have any questions before signing up.

"That would be great."

"Thanks so much again." Jack said.

"You are welcome. Bye Beemer."

We made our way over to Katie and Misty. "Well they did it- they are graduates!" I said.

"Yes yes they are. Have you guys decided on the Pet Therapy Training?"

I looked at Jack. "Yes I think we might."

"Oh good so we will see you."

"It would definitely be more fun for them to do it together. We will let you know for sure."

We exchanged numbers and emails with Katie to keep in touch. Katie actually did not live too far from us so we would often run into them at the park.

"Beemer look – there's your friend Misty." I would point and he would look and start heading over.

Long Leash

After Obedience Training, at one point not sure why we thought of it but we got a long leash, 20 feet, to take Beemer on walks so he could get to run ahead and still be on a leash and I could catch up. I would do hand signals and command "Wait" and he would always listen.

I thought it was so cool Beemer responded to hand signals. If we were coming to a corner I would say "Left" or "Right" and point and he did it. All the cars lined up at the corner would watch us as we turned. They were not sure if we were going to cross the street.

One hand signal we often did on our way home was when we got to the corner store. Most times we would cut through the parking lot, but if Beemer did any business then there was a garbage can on the corner. "Corner Beem. We have to put this in the garbage." And I would point straight ahead. Amazing that he learned what that meant and continued straight on the side walk and stopped in front of the garbage can instead of turning in the parking lot. I threw the bag in the can and we continued on our way home.

Role Model

One of our neighbors down at the end of the block had a Bichon Frise. Whenever we would walk by and the door was open, their door was a full glass door, their Bichon would bark at us as we walked by. This one day Jack was taking Beemer on a walk and saw them with a trainer on their front lawn. As they were walking by Jack saw that across the street another neighbor's Golden Lab got out and was running toward Beemer. Jack dropped the leash and commanded Beemer "Sit and Stay." Beemer did. Jack called the Golden Lab over and held his collar. The owner quickly came out to get him. "Look at that!" the owner of the Bichon said and pointed at Beemer. "We want our dog to do that." Beemer sat the whole time even though he was wagging his tail Jack said. Here the Bichon Frise was getting training and Beemer was a role model.

Once Beemer completed Obedience training we could see a world of difference. Even if people are not going to go forward with Pet Therapy or Agility it is definitely worth the time and effort to do Obedience training. You can even make it a family project as several people brought their children to class so everyone would learn the instructions. Consistency and routine is the key to success.

Pet Therapy Certification

"I really think it would be good for us to do the Pet Therapy Training. If for nothing else other than to visit my Mom."

"Okay if you want to." Jack said.

"Well Mary thought he would do really well. And everyone at my Mom's place really wants to see him."

"Yeah sure. Why not."

"I would really love to volunteer other places too, but we will have to see how it all works out."

"Yeah and if he passes the test."

"Ha Ha. He will pass. I know it. Right Beem? Tell him." Beemer just looked.

"Well it is a big commitment. Once you start you can't just stop going."

"Right."

We decided to definitely do the Pet Therapy Training. We let Katie know Beemer and Misty would be doing Pet Therapy training together.

Some Lessons for Pet Therapy Training

- Need to be able to give the command "Down" and have them lay down immediately in case of an emergency or anything drops on the floor which happens often with older people if their hands are not steady.
- Need to be able to say "Leave it" on command in case anyone dropped pills on the floor so they will not eat them.
- They need to be able to be comfortable around equipment and not knock anything over like canes, wheelchairs, or IV poles.

- They cannot jump or bolt if there are loud noises if any of the equipment is dropped like canes or bedpans.

After 8 weeks it was the day of the Test. I was a little nervous. Beemer had done well in all the practices tests but we really wanted him to pass.

It was time to celebrate. Both Misty and Beemer completed the training and passed the test.

"Oh this is so exciting." Katie said.

"Yes I am really happy. I thought I messed up that one part of giving the Down command but luckily it was ok." I said.

"Yes Cole knows you guys do it all the time."

"Next step is to sign up with the Agency. They said they will email you lists of where you can go for Pet Therapy."

"Yes then we can start our visits. I can't wait." Katie said.

"I will be happy to bring him to see my Mom and let everyone pet him."

"Maybe we will even go to visits together." Katie smiled.

"That would be wonderful. I will have to see what they have available. Since I work full time I will only be available on nights and weekends."

"Oh I see. I am available most anytime."

"Well hopefully it will work out."

"Yes I am sure it will."

"We will definitely see you if not on visits then in the park."

"Yes that's right."

We hugged Katie goodbye. "Bye Misty and Congratulations."

"Congratulations to you too Beemer."

We received an Official Therapy Pin and Certificate.

We also connected with a few of the other people in our Pet Therapy Training. One was Joey and her little Westie named Sassy. Sassy is cute as a button. Joey said she had several places lined up for Pet Therapy visits and if we were interested we could give her our email and she would put us on the mailing list and so we did.

Another person we made friends with was Terri and her dog Chaos who was also a Pit Bull mix. She handed out flyers to attend a 'Dog Walk for Cancer.' "We have this fundraiser ever year so if you would like to attend it is a great event. They have lots of activities and I also have a mailing list." We definitely signed up.

Pet Therapy is a big commitment. There is an investment of time. You have to practice and be consistent every day. In addition to the training you also have to make sure they get their shots, are perfectly groomed, and on their best behavior. There can be no jumping on anyone or barking or playing with the other dogs; all the things we learned in training. Plus once certified you need to register with an agency for insurance and need to renew yearly. After being certified and registered the biggest investment is volunteering your time. Seeing the reward of people's smiles and with making my Mom so happy we knew it was worth every penny and every second. Beemer and I were ready. "Good Ready!"

Beemer "Good Down and Stay"

Agility

We watched one of the Agility sessions one day after Pet Therapy class. It was fascinating to see the dogs go through the course and the equipment. "Do you think Beemer can do that?" I asked Jack.

"Seems kind of high for some of the equipment."

"We know he loves to jump high from day one with Bobby."

"Maybe. I just don't want him to get hurt or anything."

"Yes I agree. Well we can try it and if it doesn't work out then no big deal. I think he can do it."

In 'Intro to Agility' the instructor would introduce a new piece of equipment each week. When we first went Beemer was initially very hesitant and shy of the equipment. First up was to get him to jump up on the Platform Table. It was a 3 foot square platform about a foot high. He would touch his paw on it and decided it was not for him. "Beemer jump. C'mon you can do it." We tried to encourage him with treats but Beemer was never really enticed or motivated by treats. Later in life he did like to eat and get treats but having grown up in a shelter he never learned that initially.

"Walk him around it and let him get used to it." the instructor suggested. We actually had to pick him up and put him on it to try to get him to understand that he needed to jump up on the table. After that he was a champ. Sometimes he would jump so fast he would land on the table and then jump off the other side. Finally he got it and stayed on top. The next week he jumped up on the platform with me just pointing to it even without a verbal command first.

Next was the Dog Walk which was a 12 foot long platform, about a foot wide and 4 feet high. It reminded me of the balance beam in gymnastics. This one he did effortlessly. He just walked right up the ramp and across with no hesitation. We were amazed. We thought he might get freaked out since it was only a foot wide but not at all. He just walked right across. "That is really good." The instructor said. "Yes we are shocked."

Beemer on the Dog Walk

We practiced those with the others in the class. After a few weeks once they learned a few pieces of equipment the instructor would show you a routine and then each person would take a turn with their dog.

The A frame was tough for a lot of the dogs to climb. It was a Triangular platform 3 foot wide with slats and about 6 foot high. The dogs had to climb up and then back down the other side. They are supposed to touch at the bottom of the A frame as required. In the beginning you helped encourage them up with treats and the same on the way down.

The Seesaw which was 12 foot long and 1 foot wide and 2 foot high was the hardest for Beemer to master. He got up fine but as soon as the seesaw turned to go down he would jump right off. He did eventually get it and when he got it right we gave him extra praise. "Good boy Beem. See you can do it!" He did get better and do it reluctantly but definitely not his favorite. During his routines though at a full course run he would often run around it instead of over it.

The Tunnel was a 2 foot circumference long tube either 12 or 20 feet long. First time like most dogs do they go in and then back out. The goal is to get them to go in and then run to other end and meet them when they get out. Initially we had someone stand on each end to coax them to go thru. The command as we approached was to point and say "Go Tunnel". After a few tries, Beemer was a Pro at "Go Tunnel." He would barrel through there so fast. Beemer waited for me to get to the other end and looked so happy. It was awesome. This became one of his favorites. If we got to class early and before it started we practiced with him. If I let him off the leash he immediately headed to the Tunnel.

Beemer "Go Tunnel"

Hurdles. In the beginning the instructor only had them about a foot high until we could learn the command "Jump." We graduated to about 2 foot high. Once Beemer got going he would always jump at least a foot higher then he needed to with "Ooohs and Ahhs" we heard from the class.

Weave Poles. It was a set of 10 or 12 poles spaced apart that the dogs had to weave in and out of. This was another challenge for Beemer. We had to practice the weave poles a lot. We set up weave poles in the backyard. We used the green plastic Garden stakes. They worked great. Beemer would often skip and do two or three at a time. But when he got it right and did them all one by one it was terrific.

The Chute. Another of Beemer's favorites was the Chute or Closed Tunnel. It had an opening like the Tunnel in the front and then a collapsible nylon fabric which was closed on the back end. When they went through they could not see the end but had to run straight through. This was difficult for a lot of dogs. Many were afraid of it as they could not see through to the end and hard to get them to go in. Others would get stuck and not continue through or try to back out so the instructor would hold the end open until they got it, but for some reason Beemer loved it. Beemer would go so fast thru no one could believe and he would turn around and look as if to say "Look what I did." I was always so proud of him on that one.

Beemer really came out of his shell thru Agility. He was still not a fan of grocery bags when we brought them home but he was no longer skittish. When we would walk in we would say "Hi Beem. Yes Beemer scary bags, but they have good stuff for you." I would bring one over so he could sniff. After the Intro to Agility class we would bring Beemer every Saturday to the drop-in Agility session. When the weather was nice it was held outside, but if it was not nice then they would set up a smaller amount of equipment on the inside so they could still get their Agility run. Beemer's sweet and playful personality really shined through at Agility.

Beemer on Agility Run

Class Clown

Beemer became the Class Clown in his Agility class. Many looked forward to Beemer's turn. It was always something unexpected. He would listen to a point but always put his own twist on it.

One time in the beginning I saw Beemer was going to jump from the top of the A Frame I put my hands to my head and said "NO!" Some of the other class members held their hands over their mouth and gasped. Thankfully Beemer landed on his feet with a 'whoosh.' Everyone was relieved especially us. Looking at Jack I think Jack wanted us to quit Agility at that moment. Beemer shook it off and then started running. I called and chased him to try to get him off the field so the next person could take their turn. Beemer ran amuck on the field. He started jumping hurdles willy nilly. "Beemer!" I called. There was no stopping him as he ran through the tunnels and finished with the chute. He then ran to the sideline where all the other dogs were and he wagged his tail. That was not good but it was funny. Mary was there that day. Mary shook her head and said "That's Beemer."

After that I was afraid he might get hurt so I stood closer to the A frame and pointed to the bottom. "Easy Beem. Easy!" I would say. That worked much better. He didn't go all the way down, maybe three quarters, but at least he did not launch from the top. I was more stern in my commands and Beemer did much better covering the course.

At that point we definitely knew Beemer was not a candidate for competition. Yes he was fast enough but he always had so much fun that we did not want to take that away from him to be more disciplined. Especially since he was totally disciplined for Pet Therapy; this was his let loose time. Beemer was in Agility for fun and exercise. We were good with that.

We started coming to class early to practice with Beemer. We thought it may help him to not be so excited during class. Beemer was not always patient waiting for his turn as he watched the dogs running he wanted to join them. He would lay down and let out his signature whine. "Shh Beemer we have to wait our turn." Everyone in front of us laughed.

No one could beat the Border Collies in Agility in our class. They were so fast and did the course with precision on the equipment. Beemer loved this one guy in class named Tug. He would love to play with him and run around. Tug was the best in the class. He would go and do the course perfectly with Praise from the instructors and Kudos from all.

Then it was our turn. 'Oh Boy' I thought we can't compare to that! Beemer did Agility in his own way. Would we win the competion – no – but it really didn't matter. We had a great time and Beemer would get a different kind of Praise and Kudos. When he would jump twice as high as necessary over the hurdles, people would say "Ohhh" or "Wow look at him go". Even the instructor said. "He can jump really high." Beemer was enjoying it and to us that was all that mattered. In between obstacles Beemer would run while smelling the ground. The instructors and even Mary said "We have never seen a dog run so fast with his nose to the ground like that."

While doing our routine the goal was to get through the course fast but precise on each piece of equipment. Sometimes before getting to the next obstacle Beemer would run and do a "Spin". Sometimes when he approached the tire he would run around it instead of jumping through it. The chute was usually one of the last obstacles before the end of the routine. Beemer would go so fast and when he came out at the end he would turn around looking at everyone with his tail wagging waiting for praise and applause. He had the look that he was so proud of himself. Of course we cheered and clapped and Beemer came running back to the end of the line to wait for another turn.

We loved seeing him enjoying himself and so did most everyone else. Some people whose dogs would do the routines perfectly may not have been too happy with us. It was awesome to watch them go through. "See Beem that's what you need to do." I would say. Regardless of how Beemer did it was always fun.

Beemer came along way from that day he launched off the A frame. With practice he learned to listen and followed the course as instructed for the most part. He would still sometimes end with the chute even if he wasn't supposed to but always got a laugh and finished his turn happy.

After class we would let Beemer run out back before we left. When it was time to go I would wait for him near the gate. I would kneel down and open my arms and call him over. "Beem Come." He would come running directly at me thinking he was going to knock me over. I never moved and what he would do is whiz by me 'Physch' and then circle back and come into my arms for a hug and a kiss. Awesome. At first I thought it was because he was so fast and could not gage his momentum but then thought he was just having fun.

One day when Beemer was still running around Mary came over to us. I thought 'Aw oh' we might be in trouble.

As Mary walked over she had a smile and said "He really loves to run."

"Yes he really does. You would never know he had a broken leg."

"Really? I had no idea."

"Yes that is how they found him when they brought him to the shelter."

"Wow that is amazing. Well feel free to bring him by anytime to let loose."

"Oh he would love that. Thank you so much!"

We loved this school and all the instructors. We were so grateful we found them. They did so many wonderful things. Puppy Kindergarten was adorable. Beemer loved to see the puppies as we were leaving and they were coming in. Beemer was always so gentle with them. The instructors even volunteered their time to give Obedience Training for free for shelter dogs to help them have a better chance at being adopted. That we give total appreciation since Beemer came from the shelter. Beemer learned to listen to commands, walk nicely on a leash and his priceless gift of becoming a Therapy Dog to help others.

Bond

Through Training, Agility, Pet Therapy and Love Beemer and I developed an extremely strong bond. After his training we were very connected and in sync with one another. I would often just give hand signals with no verbal command and Beemer would understand. It started in Agility and then progressed to daily life. I would point to things or a direction of where we were going without saying anything and he would respond. I would lower my hand for down and he would do it. I would pull my hand forward and that would mean stand. I would push my palm back and he would sit. If I waved my hand towards me he would come. If I pointed to my feet he would come over and sit so I could put his leash on. Again without any words. Same with tricks. I would hold out my hand and he would give paw. I would lift my hand up and he would 'Sit Up.' When I first taught him to do a circle I would hold a treat and let him follow to do a circle and say "Circle." Now I just take my index finger and make a circle and he would turn around in a circle. I often think he would have made such an excellent companion service dog. He was very smart and learned quickly.

We were together in everything. My Mom used to say to her beloved Pepper "It's you and me against the world kid." We can totally relate to that. Both Jack and I feel like it is Beemer and us together through it all.

Chapter 7 – Friends and Family – Part 1

When Jack and I first moved into my Grandparent's house we were the youngest people on the block. Most everyone was retired and I knew them from visiting my Grandparents. Jack and I would help them if they needed a hand with things. Over time as they moved to Assisted Living or sadly if they passed away the block began to change. Younger couples or families moved in. The first was Sam who lived on one side. On the other side of our house was Sandy and Ken. And two doors down was Margie and Alan. We all became great friends. During the summer we would have barbeques almost every weekend. We would all be at our house or Sam's. Everyone would make or bring something to eat and we all had a great time. We were lucky to have so many great friends on our street.

Everyone helped everybody which was incredible whether it would be borrowing power tools or shoveling snow. I would tell other people how we all got along and many people said "I don't even know my neighbors." How sad I thought.

As other people moved in on our street we joked that Sam was like the Mayor of the block. He always went down to introduce himself when someone new moved in he invited them to the next party so we all could meet. That's how we met Kerri and Colin when they moved in next door to Sam.

Beemer's Tale

When we got Beemer, he became family to everyone. He was welcome and invited and we were so happy to take him everywhere.

<u>Visit with Mom</u>

Before moving to Assisted Living my Mom helped foster dogs at her home. She had great intentions of finding them a forever home. It turned out she quickly became attached and adopted them. She loved them and gave them their forever home. She had two; Daisy, a sweet Lab mix and Pepper, a brindle Boxer–Pit mix. My Mom had Multiple Sclerosis and as it progressed over the years she had to move to Assisted Living when my Dad passed away to get the full time care she needed. Daisy had passed away a year before my Dad and my Mom only had Pepper. It was so hard for her to have to leave her home and her faithful companion Pepper. It broke my heart. We had to take Pepper.

"Don't worry Mom, Jack and I will take her and you will know she is in good hands. Pepper will get to retire down the shore." We would give my Mom reports and updates on how Pepper was doing and brought photos which she loved. Pepper passed away several months before we got Beemer. It was really tough on us and for my Mom.

I remember the first time we brought Beemer to see my Mom at Assisted Living. We thought it would be good for her since she was so sad and missing her Pepper. We walked toward her room. Everyone wanted to pet Beemer as we walked by. When we got to my Mom's room she was sitting up in her wheelchair.

"Hi Mom! How are you?" Without any prompting Beemer immediately walked right up to my Mom and put his head in her lap. My Mom had the biggest smile. My eyes started to tear up. It was the sweetest thing for Beemer to go right over to her and make her so happy like he knew her for years.

"Aww Is this Beemer?" my Mom said and she pet his head. Beemer gave her a little tail wag.

On the next visit my Mom was in bed. I patted the bed and said "Up up Beemer" thinking he would only put his front paws up on the bed. Instead he just hopped right up on the hospital bed which was pretty high.

"Oh wow hello." My Mom said laughing. Beemer layed right down next to my Mom. She absolutely loved it.

First Bark

On May 11, 2003 we went to visit my Mom for a Mother's Day Celebration. My sister and I reserved the Day Room in the facility and we brought a tray of sandwiches, our Mom's favorite, with all the fixings and dessert.

Of course Beemer came with us. My sister and her husband and their son Mikey were going to meet us there. Our Mom is a very strong woman. She was in hospice care when Mikey was born. Once she learned she was a Grandmother she decided to stay for him. She battled the doctors and beat the odds. So today was definitely a day to celebrate.

We were all sitting at the table while Beemer and Mikey were sitting on the floor on a blanket playing with toys. All of a sudden Beemer let out a loud bark which actually startled Mikey and all of us. It was a really deep bark. Beemer stood up and the hair on his back was standing up as well.

"Did you hear that – was that Beemer?" I said. Since the first day he came to live with us Beemer never barked.

My sister and I went right over to see what Beemer was looking at and saw it was one of the male aids who was coming down the hall and stopped dead in his tracks.

"Oh! It's okay. He's friendly." I said. I am sure the aid didn't believe me. He just nodded and turned the other way. I went over to Beemer and petted his head "Good Boy Beemer Good Boy! It's okay he works here." Beemer took a step and then did a shake. Mikey laughed, one of those big belly laughs which made us all laugh along with him.

Jack came over. "Good Beem. I think he was protecting Mikey."

"Yes I think he definitely was." I said.

After the first time Beemer barked with our nephew we tried in the worst way to get him to bark again. We would bring treats to him and say "Speak. Come on Beemer you can do it." Jack and I would sit with him over and over going "Speak! Speak! C'mon Beemer. Woof Woof. Ruff Ruff." We were like two crazy people trying to sound like a dog with no success.

He just looked at us and kept giving his paw for the treat. He made cute little whiney sounds but no bark. We just laughed and gave up. I said "Okay my boy you earned it." And gave him the treat.

Beemer with Mikey at Mother's Day Celebration

One night for some reason Beemer stayed on the couch and did not come to bed. 'C'mon Beem it's bedtime." I said. He didn't budge off the couch. "Ok my good boy have a good nite." And I kissed him on his head. Jack did the same. "Nite Beem."

I awoke suddenly and nudged Jack. "Did you hear that?"

"What What – what's the matter?"

"I think Beemer just barked." I whispered. I sat up and waited. Beemer barked again.

"OMG I can't believe it."

"Wow that is a deep bark." Jack said.

I jumped out of bed and went in the living room to where Beemer was. "Hey good boy. Good boy!" I started to pet him. He was standing looking out the window. There were police cars across the street at the neighbors and then the Ambulance came. "Good boy Beemer. Good boy!" I said as I hugged him.

Jack came out.

"Look he saw the police! I really hope everything is ok across the street. That is so great he barked!"

"I never thought I would hear that." Jack said.

"I hope everyone is okay and it's nothing really serious across the street."

"Yes I am going to go check." Jack said.

We finally had our guard dog. That was one year later after his first bark with Mikey.

Ever since that day we always praised him for barking. It was rare but when he did we would say "Good boy. It's your job to watch the house."

Occasionally when strangers or a dog he would not know walked by he would bark when looking out the window. "Watch 'em Beem. Who do you see?" If it was someone he would know he would just wag his tail and do his little sweet whine. If it was someone he did not know he would let out a few barks. The hair along his back would stand up like a Mohawk. Some people said he looked like a Ridgeback. Who knows maybe he is part Ridgeback.

Going to PA

Jack's parents lived in Pennsylvania near Scranton. It was about a three hour drive. We decided to take Beemer and visit them for Thanksgiving and it was also Jack's Dad's birthday. Jack's parents also just got a new dog. A Pomeranian named Pepi. Pepi was in addition to their wire haired Fox Terrier named Daisy. We thought it would be great for Beemer since he would have some playmates.

We packed up the car. It was Beemer's first Road Trip. We watched the weather report and thought if we left right away we could make it there before the snow storm. We were good until we got to the Poconos. The snow was coming down pretty heavy and I had to drive really slow. It was definitely Beemer's longest car ride.

As we were driving I thought of Gloria Estafan going thru the Poconos. "Please let us get through ok, Please let us get through ok." That was my request. We did make it through. "Thank You God. Thank You God!" We opened the car door and Beemer jumped out into the snow. Jack's parents often had tons of snow as they lived on top of a small mountain. Beemer did his business and barreled into the house and up the stairs. It was a large bi-level. Here was a whole new house to roam around and smell. Beemer went right over to Jack's Mom who was standing there holding Pepi. Jack's Dad always went to sleep early so he was sound asleep. "Hi we made it." Jack said.

"Thank God you are here."

Beemer tried to smell Pepi in his Mother's arms." She bent over and let Beemer see Pepi."

"Hi Baby. Is this Beemer?"

"Yes this is Beemer." I said.

Daisy came right over to see Beemer. Tails were wagging a mile a minute.

"He's so cute. Come in. Come in. Shut the door and do you want something to eat?"

We had a great visit. Beemer got to run around with Pepi and Daisy. Pepi and Beemer did a marathon around the coffee table.

We would let Beemer loose to run around. His parents had a Christmas Tree Farm next door to their house. What an awesome time Beemer would have running across the field among all the Christmas trees. He would run with Daisy. So fun to watch them go. I only wished I had a video camera. Back then cell phones did not have a video option as today so it was not so easy to capture such precious moments unless you had a video camera.

The Christmas Tree Farm was perfect for running around. We thought this was Beemer's idea of heaven.

Beemer in the PA Snow and Running with Daisy

Beemer and Pepi

Beemer doing his 'Spin' with Daisy

Rolling In

On another visit to PA when the weather was warmer, we came back from running through the Christmas Tree Farm. We noticed Beemer stunk to high heaven. He disappeared amongst the trees a few times but when we called him he came running back.

"Beem what did you do?" He was just standing wagging his tail.

"He must of have rolled in Deer Poop." Jack said.

"Ewww. Oh my God Beem."

"I can't believe it as he always likes to be so clean."

"I know. Oh my well guess it is time for a bath. There's no way he is sleeping with us or anyone smelling like that."

Beemer Enjoying the Christmas Tree Farm

BFFs

Jack and Jeff were friends since they were born. Jack's family lived in an apartment over Jeff's Father's store. They played together and stayed friends even though they did not go to school together. Lauren and I were best friends in high school. Lauren actually introduced me to Jack. Lauren married Jeff and we all are still very close to this day. Lauren and Jeff adopted a little girl named Elizabeth in 2003. Beemer came to their house for parties and on occasion if we minded Elizabeth. Lauren always had cats. That was not a problem since Beemer was cat friendly. I remember their Miss Kitty who was a sweet black cat. Miss Kitty and I always did head butts together. When Beemer was there she did not come out for the festivities. Sometimes we all even spent Holidays together if possible. Lauren, Jeff and Elizabeth are always invited to wherever we are going to be and vice versa. As Elizabeth got older it was so sweet as she would always ask "Where's Beemer?" if we did not bring him. "Beemer's home but you will get to see him next time you come to our house." "Yay." Elizabeth replied. Whenever they all come to our house Elizabeth and Beemer hang out on the couch or lay on the floor together. They are BFFs. We all are. Later Elizabeth wanted a dog and they got a sweet Golden Lab mix named Army. Army and Beemer also became BFFs.

BFFs - Beemer and Elizabeth

Living with Sam

At the end of March 2005 we had our only bathroom redone. At the time Sam was single and had one of our previous neighbors and friend Keith as a roommate.

At first we talked to Sam and asked "Would we be able to use your shower and bathroom while ours is under construction? We could get a Porta Potty and just come over for showers."

"Are you crazy? Just come stay here."

"Are you sure?"

"Yes definitely."

So Jack, Beemer and I moved in Sam's spare bedroom on the first floor. The job was only supposed to take 10 days but it took a lot longer than expected. Sam loved it as Jack cooked every night and cleaned. Beemer was happy getting to hang out with his girlfriend Gizzy. They looked so cute sitting or laying on the couch together. Sam had a couch in front of the window so they both got to look out. Gizzy was a barker and whenever she would bark Beemer would jump up and look out but never joined in the barkfest.

Beemer sitting on Sam's Front Lawn

Beemer and Gizzy Hangin Out

Holidays

Beemer was always welcome to come with us wherever we were going to be for the Holiday. If we were hosting, Beemer loved the company.

My nephew Mikey always made me laugh. I would talk to him on the phone before they came for a Holiday. Mikey would say "I want to come to your house."

"That's great. We will see you this weekend for Easter. I will be waiting for you."

"You will be waiting for me?"

"Yes."

"Will Uncle Jack be waiting for me?"

"Yes."

"Will Beemer be waiting for me?"

"Absolutely. Yes. Beemer will be waiting for you."

"Happy Easter Beemer!" We would always have a little toy or a small bag of treats for him from the Easter Bunny. If we were hosting then we would tell Beemer "Mikey, Rusty and Buddy are coming to see you Beem." He would stand up on the couch and look out the window wagging his tail. "Not yet my beauty but they are coming to see you." Rusty was my sister's shepherd mix. He was older and very sweet. Beemer and Rusty got along great. Buddy was their new puppy, a mix of Burmese Mountain Dog and Rottweiler. Whenever anyone was coming over we always mentioned their names and if they were bringing their dogs. "So and So is coming to see you Beem." As soon as he would hear them pull in the driveway he would immediately stand up on the couch, look out the window, wag his tail and let out a little whine. When he saw who it was when they stepped out of the car he would fly off the couch and head right to the door. "They're here Beem." We would open the door. "Easy Beem. Go easy." Sometimes that helped and sometimes he was so excited he just flew off the top of the stairs. He always went to greet whoever came. He never jumped on anyone he just went right up to them to say hello. Of course if they brought their dogs then the hair would stand up along Beemer's back in excitement. Then it was a race to see who could get to the back yard first. Beemer always won with everyone trailing behind.

Baby Buddy, Rusty and Beemer with Mikey

Baby Buddy

If my sister was hosting the holiday then when we would be getting ready to leave we would say "Beem we are going to see Rusty, Buddy and Mikey." Beemer would get very excited and wait at the door. "Yes you're going." We wanted to make sure he knew this was not just a park ride or that he was going to be left home. Maybe it was our imagination but it seemed like Beemer knew the difference. When he got in the car he would lay down as if expecting a longer ride. When we said "Time to go to the park!" then when he got in the car Beemer would sit and look out the window until we arrived at the park.

When we went to my sister's, her one sister-in-law and husband, Fran and John, were not a fan of dogs. Whenever my sister's dogs would come over they both would get up or move away. When Beemer would come over I would see out of the corner of my eye that both Fran and John would pet Beemer when he sat by them. John really did not like dogs and yet Beemer won him over. Fran would comment "Beemer is so well behaved and calm." I smiled. "Yes. Yes he is."

Staying Over

Whenever we stayed at other people's homes Beemer always went to sleep with them at night. Unless they kicked him out he would sleep there and then come to find us in the morning to let him out.

Beemer in Bed with Jack's Brother

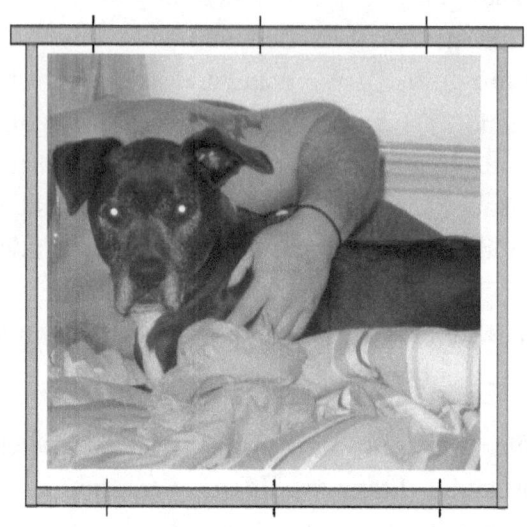

BBQs

Beemer loves when we have people over, but for some reason he never liked being confined in our garage. We set up the garage with a table and chairs so if it was raining we could still sit and eat outside in the summer for a barbeque. Jack had put gated screen doors on the front to keep out the mosquitoes. As soon as you opened the door Beemer flew out. We think maybe it reminded him of being in the shelter.

Instead Beemer would lay in front of the garage in the driveway. Because we had a stone driveway we would bring out a carpet for him to lay on instead of directly on the rocks. If it was raining we would set up a tarp extending out from the edge of the garage out to the driveway so he could lay there and not get soaked. This way Beemer was always part of the party instead of putting him in the house.

Beemer in the Driveway

Rob would come over whenever we would have a BBQ. We had balls and toys for the kids to throw for Beemer. Beemer never learned fetch to bring it back but the kids would have a great time yelling and laughing as they all chased him around the tree to get the ball or toy. They only got it back when Beemer would drop it and retreat to his 'Den' under the bushes for a rest. It was a win-win for everyone. Beemer would get exercise and the kids would get tired out.

Beemer with the Kids

One night we were sitting hanging out with Rob after everyone else left. "I think Beemer is an alien." Rob said. Jack burst out laughing.

"What? What do you mean?" I said.

"He doesn't bark and he is not like any dog I know."

"He is different. Yeah like E.T." Jack chimed in.

"Ha Ha." I said.

"He is almost like a person just hanging out with us." Rob said.

"Now that I would agree with." I said.

E.T.

Rob said Beemer was like an alien. Not like other dogs. At first we thought that was funny but then we really did notice he was different.

The "E.T." joke nickname kind of stuck whenever he would have an alien moment. Whenever we would do gardening and dig up dirt Beemer would immediately come over to smell the ground and do a little dig of his own with his paw. "My botanist like E.T. You coming to help me good boy?" One time he even picked up my plastic shovel and ran away with it. "Hey I need that. Guess you are going to do some planting of your own Beem." I laughed and chased after him.

Beemer with the Shovel

Beemer definitely had a gift for smell. Beemer loves to smell everything, but on many occasions we would catch him smelling flowers when he did not know we were looking. It was so touching as he would gently go up to them and sniff. We wanted to run and go get the camera but we knew if we did the moment would be lost. Instead it is a picture in our minds that we always remember.

Beemer had one experience with the Rose Bushes on the side of our house. Jack's Dad planted them the first time he came to our house. Beemer went up to smell the Roses but unfortunately as he moved away the side of his nose got scratched with one of the thorns. "Aww Beemer you got a scratch." We put Vaseline on it but it never went away. He had a little scar. Most people would not notice but we knew it was there.

When we went for walks in the fall it would take so long as he had to smell every leaf pile as we went along.

Gerry

I knew Gerry and her parents my whole life as her parents lived across the street from my Grandparents. When her parents were not well Gerry moved in with them to help take care of them.

When Jack and I moved in we would always go to visit them on Holidays. Once her parents passed and Gerry retired from her job she was home full time.

We brought Beemer over often for visits. Gerry loved Beemer. She so looked forward to seeing him. She would be sitting in her Lazy Boy recliner chair. She always had treats waiting for him in her pocket.

Gerry was like a second Mom to me after my Mom passed. We always included Gerry in all our celebrations and company and BBQs. We went to the movies and invited her to concerts; the ones we thought she would like.

Chapter 8 – Parks, Parades and Parties – Part 1

P is for Parks, Parades and Parties and not Pee. Those are all the places Beemer loves. Although Beemer does love peeing on all trees at the park.

We are lucky to have so many parks close by to where we live. We have three large parks. First is the Beach Park which is on the water . It was a little too far to walk to, but only about a five minute drive. It is a park in front and a beach in the back. It is the best of both worlds. This is one of Beemer's favorites.

We also have the Community Park which is just a few blocks from our street. It has a wooded area with trails, a walking track, swings and a Stage for events plus softball and soccer fields. The third is Bridge Park which is also about a five minute drive which has wooded trails and a big open field in the back.

Two blocks behind our house there is a Bird Sanctuary which is all woods and paths that lead out to the Bay and one street over is the Dock in front of the bay with a paved and rocky area where many people fish and crab.

There are lots of options to take Beemer for walks. We even have a Dog Beach. That is a ten minute drive. We rotated where we took him to give him variety.

On the weekends we would walk to the Dock and Sanctuary one day which is about 2 miles round trip and the other day we would walk to the Community Park which is 1.5 miles round trip; weather permitting of course. Beemer loves those long walks. We would walk all the way to the park and then walk thru the entire park and back home. I always brought water and a collapsible bowl in case he needed a drink.

Our route to the Community Park and back took at least an hour depending on how many people we met along the way. We would go up the street toward the Main Avenue at the front of our street. We would pass many stores along the way before we got to the park. Everyone got to know us and we would stop or wave as we passed by. First stop was the Dairy Queen. There were bushes out front which Beemer loves to smell. We continued past the Dairy Queen to the corner store and if the owners were looking out we would wave as we passed by. If both Jack and I went together I would wait outside while he went in to get whatever we needed. If no one else was in the store the owner would come outside to pet Beemer while we talked.

"How's your son doing?" I would ask.

"Great. He is doing so well in school. He wants to be a Pharmacist."

"Wow that is so great."

We would always check in with them to get updates. Next stop depending what time we went would be the Crossing Guard at the corner.

"There he is." She would always bend down to hug Beemer.

"Thanks for getting us across safely." We would say as we continued on our way.

On the next stretch of road there was a Florist. They had many plants, flowers, trees and bushes out front. "Beemer this is a no pee zone okay? No Pee. You can pee all you want once we get to the park." He always understood. He would stop and smell but never pee. One of the workers, Jack always called her our 'Beautiful Flower Lady' whenever we saw her. Margie was in her early sixties, short and sweet and her smile was priceless when she heard her endearment. She was always happy to see us and pet and hug Beemer.

"How is your puppy doing?" She had a miniature collie.

"Well she is not a puppy anymore, but she is doing good."

"I call them all puppies no matter what age."

"Have a good day."

"You too." And we were on our way.

Then we would continue and Beemer would pick up the pace in a trot as there was a long stretch where there were no stores. Across the street though was Gizzy's groomer Denise. We met Denise when we picked up Gizzy from being groomed when Sam could not get home from work on time. We started taking Beemer there to get his nails cut since she was so close by. We would always wave as we ran by. The next time we would go to Denise's she would say "I see you guys run by on your way to the park."

"Yes we always wave to you."

Denise always said "I only know one Beemer. And I have groomed tons of dogs over the years." I thought 'YES' there really is only one Beemer.

Then we would get to the corner after the Bank and I would tell Beemer 'Right' and point. We made our way down the street until the next 'Left' which led directly to the Park.

That's when Beemer really got excited. He knew we were close. "Almost there my boy." I would say. When we got to the end of the street we looked both ways and crossed and made our way into the gate of the park.

We would start walking through the park and depending on the day or time we would see all the people and dogs that were regulars. Sometimes there would be a soccer game with lots of people and animals watching on the side lines. We greeted all that seemed friendly.

"He thinks everyone is here to see him." I would say.

"And why not?" was one response. "He is so cute." "Can we pet him?" "What's his name?" "What kind of dog is he?" Some of the many responses we would receive.

And all the answers I would give "Sure. He is very friendly." "He is a rescue and a Therapy Dog." "Not sure but we think part Lab and part Pit."

When Beemer was done we would head home but always took the back streets instead of the Main Street to go home to give him different smells and make it interesting. We got to know people on the back streets too. In our town everyone has their mailbox on a post in front of the house. The only exception was if you were disabled then you could have your mailbox on your house. The mailbox posts are always a temptation for Beemer. "No pee on the mailbox." I would say. You can pee on the street pole but NOT on the mailbox." Most of the time he listened. There was this one house where an older gentlemen lived. He was very vocal about not being on his lawn or near his mailbox. I totally respected that. Of course Beemer was compelled to go there. "C'mon Beem we can't smell here. Let's go to the next house." Sometimes it was a struggle to get

Beemer's Tale 114

Beemer to go swiftly by as there were so many bushes and plants that were tempting to smell, but I would try to pass by as quickly as I could.

When it was really cold out we would drive to the park and just walk in the park.

When we went to the Sanctuary if no one was on the path I would let him off the leash. He would run all the way down the path. We said he looked like Paul Revere's last ride galloping along the path. It was so quiet you could actually hear the patter of his feet hitting the ground. If there was a log blocking the path he looked like a Gazelle as he would effortlessly jump right over.

Beemer in the Sanctuary

When we got near the Dock there was this long stretch of grass in front of the condos. I would check and if no one was at the dock I would let him off lead and point to the grass. "Stay on the grass Beem. Run." He would run the whole stretch of grass and then down to the Dock. Sometimes I would try to race him. It was more like an attempt to keep up with him. Of course Beemer always won.

Beemer at the Dock

Often we would see neighbors or friends at the park. They either drove or rode their bikes there.

"Where did you park?"

"We didn't we walked here."

"Wow that's far."

Or they would say "You walked here?"

Beemer's Tale 116

I laughed. "Yes we did."

"I can't believe how far you walk."

Other times neighbors would say

"Hey we saw you at the park when we drove by."

"Yes we go every chance we get."

If someone saw us as we were walking on our way to the park people would call out to Beemer as they passed by us. "Hey Beemer!", "Hi Beemer." or just "Beeeemer." I would smile and wave.

Beemer in the Park

The exercise from all the walking definitely helps Beemer's and our lives.

During the week we would go on shorter works depending on the weather and the time change for daylight. If I got home before dark I would take Beemer. If we knew I would be late then Jack would take Beemer during the day.

Funny how his nose knows. Whenever we drove to a park I would say "Does your nose know my smart boy where we are going?"

Beemer has a different reaction for each place when we were going in the car and he knew where. We always had the window slightly open and he would press his nose to the window so he could smell. It is fascinating how Beemer would smell and remember.

- For the Bridge Park he would take his paw and scratch at the door to get out as soon as possible.
- For the Beach Park he would have his nose glued to the window until we got there.
- When we went to the Sanctuary he would pace back and forth on the back seat until we got there.
- For the Community Park he would stand at attention as he wasn't sure if we were going to drive by as that was a common route for us to take to other places. He would wag his tail when we pulled into the parking lot.
- For the Dog Beach once we crossed over the bridge he knew we were going to the Dog Beach and he would do a circle in the back seat.

As we would go on our walks we would get to learn the neighborhood on the streets on our way to the park. We went everywhere together, walked for miles and greeted everyone we met with a smile and a tail wag.

As we walked by I noticed so many dogs just sitting in the window. I bet they wish they could join us. I wished I could bring them with us. It is so good to socialize your dog and get them familiar with being around people and other dogs and animals. Often that is not the case. Either the owners are too busy or don't make the time and the doggies remain in the window.

There was one house we went by that had a black Lab named Reilly. Reilly loved to play with his ball. Every time we passed by and Reilly and his owner were out we would stop so they could play together. Beemer would get the ball and Reilly would chase him to try to get it back. We often say how we would never have connected with all these people if it was not for Beemer. Since Beemer was trained as a Certified Therapy Dog, his calm nature helped put most all the other dogs he met at ease. He was definitely a positive influence.

El Diablo

There were several families who lived close by who spoke primarily Spanish. I took Spanish in high school. I remember a number of words and understand more than I can speak. Not like one of our dear friends Jeannie who spoke Spanish fluently. It was so fun to watch her speak with people whenever we were at restaurants, shopping, and stores. She would build that camaraderie with them as soon as she started speaking Spanish.

One sunny warm day we were walking by this house and the children, a little boy and a girl, were playing on the front lawn. As soon as they spotted us coming toward their house the children started pointing and very excitedly said "Doggie, doggie!" I smiled at them as we got closer and the children started to run over. The Mother turned around and put her hand to her chest and with a horrified look she yelled "No no El Diablo! El Diablo!" which is Spanish for the Devil. She started to run toward the children. My mind was racing on trying to remember what I could say in Spanish. First thing that came to mind was 'Amigo.' I started pointing to Beemer and saying "Mi Amigo. Su Amigo." And smiled. "Bueno. Muy Bien." The children came closer and I nodded it was okay to pet Beemer. They were so happy and Beemer of course was wagging his tail. The Mother looked relieved and I nodded. There was no way I could translate Therapy Dog. She started to say something and I raised my hand and pinched my index and thumb together and said "Un Puco Espeniol." We both smiled. "Gracias." she said. "Buenos Dias." I said and waved to the children. They both waved and said "Bye doggie."

As Beemer and I continued on our walk I thought 'The Devil' Really? If they only knew he was the absolute opposite; an Angel. And he is my Angel.

After that day every time we walked by their house I would say "Hola." If the children were out they always came over to pet Beemer. If the adults were out they smiled and waved.

<u>Friend or Foe</u>

We are cautious of people with other dogs on our walks. Often people say their dog is friendly but on occasion it turned out they weren't so friendly. Beemer had such a calm, friendly and sweet nature he would go up to everyone. Some dogs did not know how to react to him. Beemer never showed aggression in any way. Sometimes one of the dogs in the park would show aggression toward Beemer. They would try to nip at his neck or jump on him. Whenever another dog was showing aggression Beemer would just turn and walk or trot the other way as if to say "Leave me alone." Some tried to follow him but Beemer kept going.

We had a few close calls where other dogs were going to go after Beemer. Luckily we always were able to stop it before anything happened. This one time we were walking home from the Dock and these two shepherd mix dogs got out and started coming toward us. They did not look too friendly to me. I started yelling "Hey – Go Home. Go Home." And pointed in the other direction. I was hoping the owners would hear me. They kept coming. "Does anyone know who these dogs belong to?" I yelled. No one was outside. I put Beemer behind me. My plan at this point was to let Beemer loose as they were a little overweight and I knew they would never catch him. They kept coming and just as I was about to let Beemer go the owner came out. He whistled and called the dogs. They stopped. He called again louder and they started to go back toward their house. "You really need to watch them. I did not know if they were friendly." The man never said a word. Wow I thought. "C'mon Beem. We are going to be careful going by here again."

Flying

We always joked that when Beemer put his head out the window he looked like he was flying since he had his 'Flying Nun' ears blowing in the wind. He always seemed so happy. One day we were on our way to take Beemer to the Bridge Park which Beemer enjoyed. Especially since there was a long path in the woods to walk through and in the back there was a huge open field. We only let Beemer off the leash if no one was there.

As we were getting closer to the park Beemer started scratching at the door which he always did once he knew we were going to the Bridge Park. "We are almost there Beem." I said. Then Beemer put his front paws on the door handle and put his head out the window. I heard a little cry. I looked in the rearview mirror.

"Oh my God! Oh my God!" I started screaming.

"What? What?" Jack said frantically.

"Beemer - the window! Jack do something! Do something!"

His paw hit the automatic window button. I was trying to drive and press my down button for the back window while Beemer was pressing up. His neck was getting squeezed by the window. Jack tried to reach around but could not get to the button.

"Pull over. Pull over!" Jack yelled.

"I'm trying!"

I was trying to get in the right lane to pull over as fast as I could but it was a busy road. Finally I pulled over and Jack jumped out of the car. He went to the driver side passenger door and jumped in to get Beemer's paw off the button. I pressed the down button so the window opened all the way. I shut the car off and jumped out and raced over. Jack let Beemer out of the car.

"Is he ok? Oh my God is he okay?" I was shaking and crying.

Beemer did a shake. I started gently rubbing his neck. "I am so sorry my boy so sorry. Are you ok?" I hugged and kissed him. "Oh Beem I am so sorry."

"You okay Beem?" Jack said looking at Beemer. "He seems to be ok."

We let Beemer walk around a little bit before getting back in the car and offered him a drink of water.

"That was so horrible." I said.

"Very scary. My heart was racing a thousand miles per hour." Jack said.

We felt so awful as Beemer loved flying with his head out the window. Never in a million years would I have thought of such a thing. From that point on I put the window lock on.

After that day Beemer never put his head out the window again. We felt so bad. He leaned back from the window and just lifted his nose to smell the air. We tried to coax him and go slowly but he always resisted. Eventually he did come closer to the window if we had it only open an inch or so. He would then press his nose next to the glass to get a better smell. Sadly Beemer's flying days were over.

Fast as Lightning

After the car window incident the only way Beemer would fly was when he ran. He loved to be chased. He would catch the ball or toy and then run away. We never got tired of watching the kids chase after him.

This one day we went to the dog beach and it was like a movie scene. There was a pack of dogs standing near the water. Beemer ran down to the end as he never likes going in the water. He would stop right at the water's edge.

Our usual response "What Lab does not like to go in the water?" Beemer then went in his play position egging the other dogs on. They caught on and Beemer took off. He ran down the beach with all the other dogs chasing him. At one point Beemer even turned his head around and looked back to see how far they were behind him. None of them could catch him. If anyone got close he would do his "Spin" and turn around and tear off in a different direction. I really wish I had a video camera or a phone to capture that moment that day. We always said he must be part Greyhound. If it was a race he definitely would have won.

Beem on the Beach

One day we were walking down the street and saw our neighbor at the end of the block who had a new puppy. The puppy was a gray Pit Bull. So so cute. We were talking and the puppy was jumping and wanted to play with Beemer. We let them both off the leash and let them run around the lawn. Our neighbor said "I have never seen a dog as fast as Beemer. He is like lightning. He runs like the wind." Fairly soon the puppy grew tired of trying to catch up to Beemer and sat down. We joked and our neighbor said "You need to bring Beemer by every day to wear him out!"

At Bridge Park we had another movie scene and lightning moment. We let Beemer off the leash in the open field in the back since no one was there to let him run around. The area was surrounded by a fence and on the one side it faced the street. I will never forget this one day. I let him loose and tried to run after him even though I never could keep up.

There was a line of cars waiting for the light to change and as we ran along the edge of the fence one of the drivers in a car rolled down their window. They yelled "Run doggie. Run! Go go go!" I laughed out loud and waved. Too fun!

A few years later they posted signs and had security come to check to make sure you did not let your dogs off leash otherwise you would get a ticket and had to pay a fine. That sucked!

Park Visits

Every time not just sometimes but every time we went to the park people would stop us to ask about Beemer.

I would always say my usual. "Yes he is friendly. This is Beemer. He is a rescue from the shelter and he is a Therapy Dog."

"What is that?" many people asked. I, or we if Jack was with me, would explain how Beemer would visit patients and people in Assisted Living facilities.

"Wow that is so great." Or "Keep up the good work Beemer." I was surprised at how many people did not even know what Pet Therapy was or that it even existed.

People of all ages and especially children would come over. The children would run over and ask if they could pet him. Many times the parents would seem a little leery but I would immediately tell them "It is ok. He is a Therapy Dog." Instantly you could see the relief on their faces. I would ask the children if they had a pet and they would tell me about their dog or cat. I would point to Beemer's feet and tell them "Well Beemer loves to walk. He always has his sneakers on." They would giggle and laugh.

Beemer Always has his Sneakers On

Across from the park on one of the side streets we met Laura and her brother Jake. Laura was so happy to see us every time we walked by. She would encourage her brother to come to pet Beemer. Initially Jake was very shy and only stood and watched. "Come over Jake and pet him." Jake just shook his head.

"That's okay. Maybe next time." I said.

"I want a dog so bad, but my parents don't want one."

"Well it's a lot of responsibility."

"I told them I would take care if it."

"That is great. But when you are in school your Mom or Dad will still have to help."

After a few months of seeing us Jake did finally come over. He had the biggest smile petting Beemer.

One day the parents were outside when Laura came running over. Her parents walked over and met Beemer. I explained he was a rescue, went through training and is a Certified Therapy dog. After that the whole family would see us and wave or come over for a pet. Eventually they did get a dog. A terrier mix smaller than Beemer; her name was Gracie. Whenever we saw them Laura would bring Gracie over to see Beemer. I always thought Beemer helped change the parent's minds on the positive impact of having a dog.

We did this routine for years. It was an hour well spent as in addition to exercise for both Beemer and I and Jack if he was able to join us, to make someone smile or feel better along our way even for a second was so great. Beemer made not only us feel better but did this for everyone he met on a daily basis.

Parties at Sam's

Beemer got to meet the rest of the neighbors at Sam's house. Sam's yard was the meeting place as he had a huge yard with a large deck and built in swimming pool. Everyone would make something food wise and bring it like a Pot Luck Dinner. It was great.

This one time Sam decided to put Beemer in the pool. "Let's see if he can swim." Sam said.

"I don't know if he is going to like it." Jack said.

Turned out Jack was right. Beemer did not like it at all; he swam immediately back and got right out. Beemer did a shake and ran to the grass area as far from the pool as possible.

"What kind of Lab are you that you don't like the water?" Jack said. Everyone laughed.

Ever since that day Beemer would not go close to the pool. We would call him over. "Come over Beem. Sam won't put you in." It took Beemer several years of coaxing so he would come over if we were sitting on the edge of the pool to come by us. He usually just layed down on the towel we brought him that we put down on the grass in the shade and he hung out with Gizzy.

When kids would come over to Sam's then they would have a great time chasing Beemer around.

Beemer always knew when Sam was having a party. He would look out the window and see all the cars pull up and the people go over to Sam's house. Every time we went to the door Beemer would go to jump off the couch. I would raise my hand and say "Not yet Beem. Don't worry you are going to the party." Then he would relax and patiently wait. When we were ready "Okay Beem. Party time." He would fly off the couch and go right to the door. He really knew where he was going. We would open the gate and he would gallop over to Sam's gate leading to the back yard. We laughed as we walked over to let him in.

Beemer in Sam's Yard

Block Party

For several years we had block parties. We would apply and have the street shut down for the day. Everyone made something and we set up big tables in the middle of the street where everyone would bring their food.

We always kept a leash on Beemer as we did not want him to think it was ok to go in the street without a leash.

That was one of our biggest rules. "No street without a leash." He was always so good with staying on the lawn and the property. Yes on occasion he would go ALL the way to the edge, but he never stepped off.

One of the people on our block was actually in a band so he would play with his band every year. It was a great time for all. Even the older people on the block would come and sit out for awhile which was great to get everyone out and socialize. We felt so lucky to live on a great block with so many wonderful people. One man Chuck at the end of the block was a volunteer for the First Aid Squad. It was great to have that connection if ever needed. So many people never really know their neighbors and here we got to know them all; old, young, children, pets and all.

House Party

After a few years Margie and Alan had a son Alan Jr. Sandy and Ken decided to move to a bigger house. Sandy and Ken had inside cats so Beemer never really got to meet them. I remember their one cat Gracie was so cute. She was grey and white and loved to eat Potato Chips. After Sandy and Ken moved they had a son, Kenny. Margie and Alan also moved to a bigger house around the block so they were still close by. We all stayed friends even after Sandy and Ken and Margie and Alan moved. Over the years the barbeques continued and the kids loved chasing Beemer around along with Margie and Alan's dog Rosie who was an Australian Shepherd. We were always welcome to bring Beemer to their homes for parties just as we were pet friendly and they brought their dogs to our house.

Parades and Events

We took Beemer everywhere since he was so well behaved. Give him a towel or blanket, fresh bowl of water and treats or a bone and he was happy. He was so happy to be there and hang out instead of being left home. We always felt so guilty when we did have to leave him home.

We went to all the Parades up the corner. Memorial Day, Fourth of July, Halloween, and Spirit Parade. We dressed him up or put on a bandana and he was ready to go. We saw all the neighbors there and often would invite friends and family to come to our house and then go to the parade. We would get breakfast before or lunch afterward and enjoy.

Beemer's Tale 132

Beemer at the Halloween Parade and Other Parades

At the beginning of the Baseball Season the Local Stadium had 'Bark in the Park' day where you could bring your dogs and watch the game. We went to 'Bark in the Park' and shared Hot Dogs with Beemer.

Finding Treasures

Over the years as we walked with Beemer we would find treasures. We found loose change, sometimes a dollar bill or two and some small pieces of jewelry. We always put whatever we found in a cup. When it would get full we would count it out and when it was enough we would buy Beemer a steak. "Beem you bought your own dinner." Or sometimes treat him to ice cream. That is Beemer's money.

We would also find sea glass on our Dog Beach visits and that went in a glass jar.

"Look how pretty Beemer. You helped us find all of this." He just sniffed the jar.

Beemer is our Treasure.

Chapter 9 – Grooming

From the day we brought Beemer home he NEVER had a bathroom accident in the house. Even if he had to go during the night he would wake us up and go to the back door.

<u>Getting Washed/Shower</u>

As part of Pet Therapy we had to groom and wash Beemer before visits. Beemer loved being clean so it was not a problem, but Beemer was never a fan of the water. Jack always made his joke "Beemer what kind of Lab are you who doesn't like the water?"

Beemer was not happy about the washing process whether it be a bath in the house or outside but as soon as it was over he loooooooved being dried off and pampered. After drying him with several towels we would drape one over his back. He looked like a race horse as he walked to go lay down. My 'Black Beauty' or My 'Seabiscut' I would call him. He always got special treats afterward for being so good. Once he was dry we would then brush him. He was so patient and really enjoyed it.

Beemer after his Bath

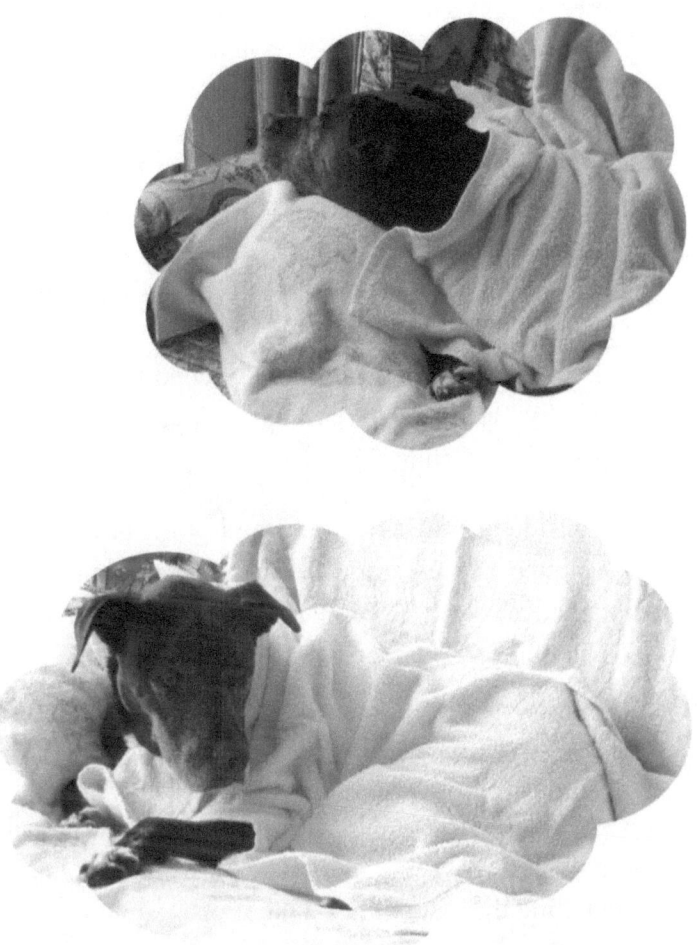

Every week Beemer would let me brush his teeth and never resisted. Teeth are so important. Sometimes he would put his paw on my hand. "Beem you are helping me my good boy." I said to Jack "Beemer was trying to brush his own teeth."

Beemer's Tale 136

Help is on the Way – Lion's Paw

Beemer always knew when we were trying to help him. It made me think of the story of the Lion's Paw.

One time we went on our walk and someone planted cactus in front of their mailbox post. Before I could catch him he went too close and "OMG" I exclaimed. He kept shaking his head and licking his nose trying to get the spikes off. I was so upset. I said "Come on Beem. I got to get you home." Luckily we were only a block away. When we got there I yelled to Jack. "Come and sit by Beemer." Alarmed Jack came over "What happened?" "Cactus."

I ran inside as fast as I could and got a bowl of water and a pair of tweezers. When I came back out I explained to Jack. "People planted cactus in front of their mailbox. Beemer got too close before I saw it. I am so sorry Beem." I bent down and started to work on Beemer. Beemer was a complete and utter Angel as he let me pull out all of the Cactus spikes that were stuck all around his nose and on his tongue. It was so hard to do and yet he sat there like the Lion with the spike in his paw letting the little mouse take it out.

Another time when we got home from our walk I noticed Beemer was walking funny. It looked like he was trying to shake something off his foot. "What's the matter B?" I walked over and picked up his leg. His whole back foot was covered in tar. "On No!" And every other curse word I could think of entered my head. There must have been a pot hole they filled in and I did not notice. I ran in the house and got a bucket of warm water and baby shampoo. I went outside and had

Beemer stand with his tarred foot in the bucket. I got a washcloth and just kept gently rubbing his foot to try to loosen the tar. I gave him breaks in between. It took over an hour and my beauty never once ran away or tried to have me stop. Finally all the tar came off. Needless to stay Beemer got tons of cookies and then steak bites that night with his dinner as a reward.

Similar incidents occurred with gum but luckily not as bad as the tar. Beemer just always had a remarkable sense of when you were trying to help him. And we did - always.

When it was time to have Beemer's nails cut we started out taking him to Pet Smart so he could walk around the store first and then get his nails cut. When it was time for his annual check-up at the Vet they would cut his nails. Later we took Beemer to Gizzy's groomer Denise. Since Denise was only down the road we could walk Beemer there. When Beemer got older he would sometimes pull his front left paw back a little when Denise was cutting his nails and give a little squeak. We think that was the leg that was broken.

"It's okay Beemer. It will be over quick and then we get to go to the park and then get ice cream."

"That sounds good. You are lucky Beemer." Denise said.

"Would you like us to bring you some?"

Denise laughed. "I am good thanks. Beemer can have mine."

Just like a child we encouraged Beemer with rewards.

Coats, Shirts and Sweatshirts

When the weather got cold we noticed Beemer shivered. He did not have a heavy coat of his own and had hardly any hair on his belly.

"I think Beemer needs a coat. He's cold." I said to Jack

"Where do you go for that?"

"I saw dog stuff in the Lands End catalog."

His first coat was bright yellow. We thought it looked great on him. Plus it just happened to be the High School colors – black and gold. It was fleece on the bottom and water resistant on top so it was great for snow and rain. "Beemer you look awesome!" We took lots of pictures. He never tried to take it off or balk from the first time we put it on. Beemer never minded wearing it; he loved his new coat. On our walks everyone would comment on it.

"Great coat where did you get it?"

"We ordered it from Lands End."

"Looks perfect on him." "He looks so handsome." "He's so cute with his coat on." were some of the compliments.

Beemer's First Coat

For really cold nights I took some of my old sweatshirts and cut them based on the shape of the coat. We would put it on and then he would snuggle down on the couch for a snooze.

Beemer Snugglin and Hanging out in his Sweatshirt

We also got Beemer a blue and gray striped sweatshirt with a hood. One day we put it on before going to the park. We couldn't believe the reaction from everyone and all the kids at the park. You would have thought Beemer was a celebrity. They all crowded around him. "Ooh look at him. I love his sweatshirt. Where did you get it? He is so cute. What's his name? Can I pet him? Aww he is adorable. What kind of dog is he? How old is he? He has white feet – You should call him Sox."

From the older kids passing by on bikes. "You look awesome dude. Cool hoodie doggie."

I always explain "Beemer is very friendly. He is a rescue from the shelter and he is a Certified Therapy Dog."

"Really? Aww that is so great. Rescues are the best."

"Yes they really are and seem to know they have a good home. Tell anyone you know who wants a pet to adopt from the shelter."

Little did they know that to us Beemer is a celebrity. On a daily basis people stop to see Beemer every time we go out. The day of the sweatshirt 'debut on the runway' was more than usual, but we always have people comment or want to pet him. Everywhere we go everyone knows and remembers his name. We laugh that they have no idea what our names are and that is how it should be. Beemer is the star.

Chapter 10 – Food – Anything Goes

We would feed Beemer twice a day. Once in the morning around 9 AM and then dinner at around 6 PM. We would mix in a little bit of leftovers with his dry dog food like Rob used to do and Beemer loves it.

In addition we shared our meals with Beemer. On weekends it was a thing since I was home where we would say time for "Lunch!" Beemer learned what that meant. We would either go for our walk before or after lunch. But when it was time for us to have lunch he always got a taste.

We also shared a taste at our dinnertime. We tended to eat later depending on what time I got home from work. Since Beemer usually had his dinner around 6 PM we thought it was ok to give him a snack before bedtime. We said we are on European time as we would usually eat around 8 PM. As we brought our plates to the table I would say "It's time for the Midnight Buffet Beemer" just like on a cruise. We would give him a taste of what we were having as long as it was something he liked or could have. We fed him with a fork for late dinner. He would eat so gently off the fork. If it was something he loved he would "Bite" a little harder on the fork. "Easy Beem. We'll give you more." If we were having something he could not have then we would give him a slice of cheese so he was included. They say you should make pets do a trick for food or a treat and in the beginning we would ask for his paw. Over time Beemer was always so good so we stopped asking him.

Beemer would make the cutest "Chomp Chomp" noise when we gave him something like spaghetti. So fun to watch him eat.

Snacks are always fun. He loves Cheese Doodles and Popcorn. We would throw them and he would catch them in the air or sometimes miss. We loved to hear him "Crunch."

Whenever we had Chinese Food or Sushi we would give him tastes and he would eat right off the chopsticks. Sushi was right up his alley. Fish which was good for him plus he loves it. For dessert Beemer loves the "Fortune Cookies." I would get the Fortune and he would get the Cookie. 'Crunch Crunch." I work with people from all over the world. One of my friends explained that in their Chinese Tradition you always offer the best food to your elders first. We always gave Beemer the best food from our plate thinking he deserves the best.

Beemer Enjoying a Taste

Beemer loves Pork Chops. Jack would make Pork Chops and actually they are very lean so we thought that was a plus. I would say "Pork Chop Pork Chop Beem that's what's for dinner." Just like Peter Brady on the Brady Bunch I gave my best impression "Pork Chops and Applesauce." Beemer enjoyed pork chops whether they were Shake 'N Bake or done on the Grill. We never gave him the bone though. We were always cautious of letting him chew on bones from steak or pork chops or ribs.

Beemer loves soup. When we had soup we would put a little in his bowl and he would lick all the broth first and then eat the meat and veggies left in the bowl.

Hot Dog

> Beemer loves Hot Dogs. Whenever Jack would cook them on the grill Beemer would stand close by smelling the aroma. Beemer always got his own. We would cut it up and put it on a plate without the bun. I would bring the plate over and say to Beemer "Hot Dog" just like George Bailey from "It's a Wonderful Life".

McDonald's

> Sometimes on the weekend we would take Beemer to McDonald's. Since he was like our kid we would go and order him his own burger and share our fries with him. We would eat together in the car and then get out to walk on the grassy area. If it was not nice out we would get take-out and bring it home for all of us to enjoy. I would always say to Beemer. "McDooooonald's – we are getting McDooooonald's." Like Eddie Murphy did from one of his stand-up shows. I thought Eddie Murphy was hilarious when he did that

routine. Beemer got to know what that meant and would get excited.

Take Out Delivery

When we ordered Take Out and had it delivered Beemer sometimes would come to the door or would stay on the couch and look out the window. He never barked when they came for delivery. We let Beemer smell the food when we brought it in.

"Smell good Beem? You are going to get some."

Initially we always shared ours with Beemer. Then after awhile we got him his own. We ordered off the Kids Menu.

Take Out - Pick-Up

On the corner of our street there was a strip mall with several take out places. We felt so lucky that we could just walk to the corner for dinner or lunch. We would call ahead and then all three of us would go for a walk to pick it up.

"Beemer we are going to get 'Lunch'." I would say. He was very excited. When we got to the corner he slowed down a bit to smell the bushes on the side. Then we would head toward the stores. He loves walking on the sidewalk in front of all the stores. His nose would take in all the good smells. Today we were going to pick up a Sub for lunch. First we would pass the Chinese Take Out. We always waved to the owner. She was so sweet and waved back and was so happy to see us even if we were not getting Chinese. The door was always open and sometimes Beemer would peek his head in and try to go inside. "Not there Beem. We are going further down." He would continue his walk with a "Pep in his step." Next was the Pizza place. Beemer loves Pizza. "Nope not here either. Keep going." Whenever anyone opened the door Beemer was ready to go in. Next was the Taco Place. "Not today Beem. Next time we will get you a Pork Quesadilla." People would be sitting at tables near the window and look and point as we passed by. Often Beemer would look in the window. So cute. "Next one Beem." We finally arrived at the Sub Shop. There was a grassy patch on the side of the building with bushes so Jack would walk Beemer over there as I would go inside to pick up the Sub. When I came out they were waiting. "Beem – I got lunch!" He would trot over and I would let him smell the bag. We made our way back across the stores with Beemer wagging his tail. We headed home with Beemer and our Sub. We would cut him a slice and he would get all the ham and cheese from his slice and no bread.

Dairy Queen

I often took Beemer up the corner for Dairy Queen for a small cup of vanilla. We would wait in line and everyone would ask about him and pet him. "He loves vanilla ice cream." I would say. Once we paid we stepped to the side and I would give him a taste right away with the spoon. "Oh how cute. He eats so nice." People enjoyed watching Beemer eat his ice cream.

Chapter 11 – Therapy Visits – Part 1

Because I worked full time we were only available to go nights and weekends for Therapy Visits.

We had to register annually with an association to do pet visits. Beemer's school was associated with and recommended an official dog therapy organization to apply to for certification and insurance.

You were required to send them a copy to confirm Beemer had all his shots. You also sent in a picture. Initially they sent you a "Welcome Packet" which included a special leash and collar with a tag which was a little red bone with white letters that said "I am a Therapy Dog" for Beemer to wear when you brought him on visits. This way all the dogs would look uniform and easy to identify as a Therapy Dog with the leash. It was red with white dog bones on it. They also sent a badge to wear with Beemer's picture and name on it and your name as the handler. We also added Beemer's Therapy Pin to the badge.

I was the designated handler but most times Jack came with us for support. The agency also sent a mailing list monthly of all the places that were available for visits. Besides bringing Beemer to visit my Mom which she loved, we started first with going to other Assisted Living Facilities. Each site had a designated Captain who coordinated the Pet Therapy Visits. If you were interested in visiting then you would contact the Captain to get on the list and get the details for the visit. Beemer's calm demeanor was definitely an asset for Pet Therapy.

Beemer was always so funny about taking pictures. "I think he is camera shy." I said to Jack. Every time we would take the camera out he would put his ears back and we could never seem to get a good picture up close for his badge picture. We would have to sneak and try to get a shot when he wasn't looking.

When Jack went to the Town Office to renew Beemer's license he gave the Rabies shot and Beemer's Certified Therapy Card. The lady at the office said "Oh you are one of those people." What? Really? Not sure what that was supposed to mean. Seems a shame at her reaction but we were proud to be one of 'Those people.' Not sure what was happening in her own life but we felt to help others in any capacity is priceless. Maybe she needed a Pet Therapy visit.

<u>Beemer's Gift</u>

>Beemer had a gift of sensing when people did not feel well even before his Therapy Training. On many occasions he would lay down next to me or Jack if we didn't feel well.

>We had an L shaped couch and Beemer liked to lay on the lounge side which was along the windows so he could look out. One time when my back was bothering me I layed on the other end of the couch on my side. Beemer got up and came over behind me and layed down to support my back. So sweet. It felt good with the pressure and he was warm.

>Jack came in and said "How are you feeling? Where's Beemer?" Beemer poked his head up from behind me.

>Another time I was sitting on the couch and I had a belly ache. Beemer came over and laid his head on my tummy. Of course I felt better.

Beemer also did this for others. One time we were away for the weekend and our neighbor Sam was minding Beemer. When we came back he told us how his girlfriend was not feeling well and was laying on the couch most of the weekend. Beemer laid beside her in the same way putting his head on her tummy. She was not a big fan of dogs, but she was okay with them. She never had one of her own growing up. Beemer stayed beside her in comfort. "He was so sweet. He was so calm and layed so still. I could just pet him and drift off to sleep. When I woke up he was still there." Sam's girlfriend said.

Beemer Providing Comfort

Knew the Difference

It was amazing to us how Beemer knew the difference from when it was fun time and when it was work time.

When we went on our Pet Therapy visits we would say. "Time to go to Work Beem." He would jump off the couch and wait at the door. He is always calm and sweet and senses the needs from the people he visits. We take him to the park afterward as a reward. "We are going to the Park Beem." If we were going to school we would say "We are going to school Beem." When we went to Agility or to Parks that was his time to cut loose and have fun and he did.

Home Visits

We often would visit people at their homes if they could not get out.

Therapy At Home – Blood Pressure

Like the commercial where the man cannot get out of the chair; that was life for Jack some days. Beemer was motivation to get out of the chair regardless of how you were feeling to go for him.

Jack had a family history of high blood pressure. Both his Mother and Father had high blood pressure. His father had a stroke as a result. Luckily Jack's Dad made a full recovery. When Jack started to not feel well we went to the doctor and they prescribed blood pressure medication. Jack unfortunately inherited it from family genetics. Jack was on medication for years.

After getting Beemer, Jack would make an effort to take Beemer for a walk. During the day when I was not there Jack would tell me how Beemer would make a point of knowing he wanted to go for a walk. Many days Jack would not feel up to it but then he would force himself to go for Beemer. Sometimes they would only go up the block and back or sometimes around the corner.

"I actually felt better after we came home." Jack said.

"That is awesome." I replied

Jack actually lost some weight from walking every day. We went back regularly for checkups and the Doctor saw a difference in Jack's pressure.

"I think we can monitor it and I am going to decrease the medication." the Doctor suggested. Over time Jack's pressure became regulated at a normal level. As science has proven the benefit of pets and exercise - here is another testimony. Jack lost weight from walking every day with Beemer, felt better and was able to get totally off the blood pressure medication. Beemer helped him immensely. Beemer's Therapy Visits started at home.

Gerry

We would always call Gerry before we came over. She would tell us to just come in so she did not have to get up to open the door. Gerry would be sitting in her Lazy Boy recliner. Beemer would go right over with a tail wag and sit and give his paw without asking. He knew she always had treats for him in her pocket. Gerry would laugh and get such a kick out of that. After treats he would then go and claim his space on the couch.

Beemer giving Paw

When Gerry got ill we helped take care of her and bring her to Doctor Appointments. Beemer's visits were even more important. It was something to look forward to and cheer her up. Gerry was one of Beemer's first Home Pet Therapy Visits.

Assisted Living Facilities

When we would go to visit the Assisted Living Facilities they would often tie in visits to holidays or times of the year and we dressed in costume to make it more festive. We would provide a bio for the host to announce us as we walked in so the residents would know who we were.

All the dogs would line up in the hall until they were called. The people most of the time would be sitting in a circle and after you were called you would walk around the circle so that each person could see you and your Therapy Dog.

Beemer Working as a Therapy Dog

Beemer had a costume or bandana he wore for every holiday and occasion including Valentine's Day, St. Patrick's Day, Springtime, Memorial Day, SummerFest in the Park, Block Parties, Easter, Fall time, High School Spirit Parade, Halloween, Wintertime, Christmas and Tree Lightings. Beemer never minded wearing his bandanas or getting dressed up. He wore it in pride.

Beemer's Tale 154

Beemer's Bios

Here are a few of Beemer's Bios which we used over the years.

Happy Howl-A-Ween

We always picked a duo theme.

Lois Lane and Superman

I dressed in a navy blue suit and even had a pill box hat from my Grandmother to look like Lois Lane. Of course Beemer was Superman equipped with his S shield on his chest and a red cape.

Next up is Beemer AKA Superman with Lois Lane.

He can run faster than a speeding bullet

Nose more powerful than a vacuum

He is able to leap stairs in a single bound

Look out in the park – it's a bird it's a plane it's Beemer – Superman!

Like Superman, Beemer was found by the side of the road and adopted from the shelter. Beemer is a Lab Mix and is a great visitor who has been a Therapy Dog for the last X years.

Beemer loves everyone – adults, children and all animals. He is even friends with the neighbor's cat!

Again like Superman – Beemer stands for Truth, Justice and the American Way!

Bee Keeper and 'Beem' the Bumble Bee

I had a tan jumpsuit and made a hat with netting to look like a Beekeeper. Beemer had his black and yellow striped Bumble Bee costume. He truly looked adorable.

Next up is Beemer AKA A Bumble Bee with his Bee Keeper.

He loves to smell the flowers, but has never given a sting.

He flies around the park and the beach enjoying wherever he goes.

Like a Bumble Bee who produces honey, Beemer is so sweet. Beemer is a shelter rescue – he was found by the side of the road with a broken leg. You would never know it now by the way He loves to run.
Beemer is a Lab Mix and is a great visitor who has been a Therapy Dog for the last X years.

He loves everyone - adults, children and all animals. He is even friends with the neighbor's cat!

Again like a Bumble Bee - Beemer tries to spread sweetness wherever he goes.

Yappy Valentine's Day

Beemer wore his red and white bandana and I was also dressed in red.

Next up is Beemer. Just as Cupid makes a perfect match for love – Cupid must have been watching as Beemer was adopted from the shelter when he was about 6 months old. Beemer is a perfect match!

Beemer was found by the side of the road with a broken leg. You would never know it today as Beemer runs like the wind in the park and on the beach.

Beemer is a Lab Mix who has a big heart and has been a Therapy Dog for the last X years. Beemer loves everyone - adults, children and all animals. He is even friends with the neighbor's cat!

Beemer is the Perfect Valentine – He loves to smell the flowers and he is so sweet. Beemer loves to go for long walks and even cuddle on the couch!

Merry Christmas

Beemer wore his Christmas bandana and I would where my Christmas Vest my Mom had given me. Think of the Ugly Sweater contest and that was it. All kinds of sequins and beads but it is very festive.

Next up is Beemer who is like one of Santa's Elves.

He loves to Tinker with Toys, Smell the Evergreens and Run in the Snow.

His favorite places are the park and the beach - spreading cheer wherever he goes.

Beemer is a Gift that keeps on Giving. With a wag of his tail and sniff of his nose he brings a smile to everyone he sees. Beemer is a shelter rescue – he was found by the side
Of the road with a broken leg. You would never know it now by the way he loves to run.

Beemer is a Lab Mix and has been a Therapy Dog for the last X years.

He loves everyone - adults, children and all animals. He is even friends with the neighbor's cat!

Again like Santa and Santa's Elves - Beemer spreads Good Cheer and Sweetness wherever he goes for the Holidays and Always.

Jolly Beemer

Happy Easter

Beemer wore his Easter Egg colored bandana and I would wear a pink or purple shirt and bunny ears.

> *Here comes Beemer Cottontail, running down the Bunny Trail, Hippity Hoppity Beemer's on his way.*
>
> *Beemer is a shelter rescue – he was found by the side*
> *Of the road with a broken leg. You would never know it now by the way he loves to run and even hop on over when he sees a dog or someone he knows.*
>
> *His favorite places are the park and the beach - spreading sweetness wherever he goes.*
>
> *Beemer is a Lab Mix and has been a Therapy Dog for the last X years.*
>
> *He loves everyone - adults, children and all animals. He is even friends with the neighbor's cat!*
>
> *Like the Easter Bunny, Beemer brings a gift to every girl and boy. With a wag of his tail and sniff of his nose he brings a smile to make your Easter Bright and Gay.*

Beemer really did have a Cottontail as the tip of his tail was white.

Beemer's Tale 160

Yappy Holidays to All!

Highlights

We had so many wonderful visits it is hard to capture them all but here are a few highlights on some of our visits.

While we were waiting in the hall to be called in, Beemer sat next to a Doberman and her handler. The elevator opened and one of the staff started to walk out of the elevator. When she saw us she froze. She was holding a tray of food to deliver to one of the rooms. "It's okay they are friendly." I said. She didn't move. The elevator doors were dinging as they were trying to close and she was half in and half out. "Really it's okay." Neither Beemer nor the Doberman barked or jumped up to try to get the food. They just sat and looked as they are trained to do. I waved to the staff member to come out and she finally took a step out and walked quickly by. It was kind of comical but felt bad as she was apparently afraid of dogs. Especially a Doberman and a black Lab/Pit mix. They were not the small fluffy kind.

It was finally our turn and we were making our way through the group of residents. We came over to one man and I said "Hello. How are you? This is Beemer."

The man petted him and then asked "So what do you give the dogs to make them so calm? Do you medicate them?"

I wanted to laugh out loud but didn't. I just smiled and said "No. They are very well trained."

"Really? None of my dogs were ever so good."

"Well Beemer has done a lot of training and even received the Canine Good Citizen Award. He always has a very calm nature and is very sweet. He loves everyone."

"I can see that." He replied.

Another time we went and this one woman was so excited to see the dogs. When we came over I introduced Beemer and she said "Oh I just love him. His white feet are so cute." Her hands were very shaky and Beemer just sat and let her try to pet him.

"Yes we tell everyone he is ready to go as he always has his sneakers on." That made her laugh and I was so proud of Beemer. He was used to shaky hands as that was a condition my Mom also had, but still he did it and made her day.

One valuable lesson we learned on our visits with Beemer is that everyone has a story to tell and it is so important to share. This was especially true on our visits to the Assisted Living Facilities where people are in their 'Golden Years.' So many people including their own family do not want to be involved but these people know so much history and we find their stories fascinating.

One example was one lovely lady, Denise, who lived across the hall from my Mom. Her daughter would always come over and see my Mom before she left visiting her Mom. She would pet Beemer and say "He is so sweet."

"Would your Mom like to see him?" I asked.

"Sure absolutely."

We brought Beemer over and introduced ourselves. We found out that Denise was actually one of the New York City Rockettes. Can you imagine?

"That is so amazing. I took dance lessons and love to dance, but to be a Rockette you must have been terrific."

Denise smiled. "Well I loved the whole experience."

We always brought Beemer over for a visit whenever we came and Denise would tell us stories of her life as a Rockette and show us pictures.

"You are absolutely beautiful. And still are." I said.

How many people can actually say they know a Rockette? We were honored.

One of my Mom's roommates was 99. You would never have guessed her age. She looked maybe early 70's at the most. Her name was Helen. My Mom introduced us. "So nice to meet you." I said.

"And who is this handsome fellow?" Helen asked.

"This is Beemer." I brought him over so she could pet him.

"He is so nice."

"Thank you. Yes we are very lucky."

"So did your Mom tell you how I got in here?"

"No we only spoke briefly on the phone before we came."

"Yeah it was something. I was playing basketball with my friends and I slipped and fell. Had to get a hip replacement. I knew I should have bought those new sneakers."

"Oh wow. Well I am sure you will recover fast. Beemer always has his sneakers on." I pointed to Beemer's feet. Helen looked over.

"I see that! Good boy. Nothing beats a great pair of sneakers." Helen smiled a big smile. "And nothing beats a great smile like yours. Still have all my own teeth."

"Thank you so much. How wonderful. So basketball – how did you start to play?"

"I love it. I have been playing my whole life. I can't wait until I can get back out on the court."

"That is really terrific."

I was totally amazed. I thought no one will ever believe me - 99 and basketball? Helen's my idol.

On one of my visits as I drove up the driveway I saw all kinds of trailers parked out front. I had to park on the side. As I got to the top of the stairs to walk in there were people outside and said "Hi. Are you visiting someone?"

"Yes I am here to see my Mom."

"Okay just go in quietly. They are currently filming."

I found out they were filming for the HBO Series 'The Sopranos.' In the show this was where Tony placed his

Mom. I did not get to see Tony himself, but did get to see Paulie Walnuts standing at a distance. Very cool. I told my Mom and everyone all about it.

When Beemer, Jack and I went to visit my Mom sometimes my sister would also bring Mikey at the same time. We would all walk in together and as we made our way to our Mom's room you could see how everyone smiled and lit up. We always stopped and talked to people and let them see Mikey and Beemer. Mikey would run ahead like he owned the place. Everyone knew him from coming every week. Then we finally arrived at our Mom's room. We would have a great visit and lots of laughs. Our Mom would often say before we left "Everything is more fun with Mikey and Beemer." She is one hundred percent right.

Beemer and Mikey

Support Dog Walk for Cancer and Other Events

We went every year to support the Dog Walks for Cancer since 2004. Terri in our Pet Therapy class handed out flyers for the first one we attended. Ever since then we were on the mailing list and received the notice for when they were having the next event.

The event was held at the County Park that was about 20 minutes from our house. That was another great spot for walking, sniffing and fun for all.

I remember our first one. We thought it would be great to go support a good cause. We mentioned it to our neighbor Kerri, who was pregnant with her first little one. Kerri and her husband Colin lived next door to Sam. We actually had a connection with Kerri from the past. Her Dad was from the same town I grew up in up North and Kerri's Mom was from the same hometown Jack lived in when we met. Funny coincidence or as we say it is life connections.

Kerri said "That sounds great. I will bring Mugsy." Mugsy was a cute little Pug who Beemer knew. Beemer and Mugsy met at one of the parties at Sam's house. We decided to all go together. It was a sunny hot day that day. You would make a donation or have sponsors to contribute depending on how far you walked.

They had so many activities:

- Coin Toss – as you were driving in you would toss coins in a bucket as a donation.
- Agility Demonstration – they set up an area with some of the Agility Equipment. Our school would do a demonstration with trained dogs so people

could see what it was like in case they wanted to sign up.
- Blessing for the Dogs – they would have medals you could purchase and then have a spokesperson come out and do a blessing for all the dogs. We bought Beemer a medal and after the blessing we attached it to his collar. He was blessed and we already knew we were blessed to have him.
- Tic Tac Toe with the Dogs – they had a section set up like a big Tic Tac Toe board. You would sign up and then stand in one of the squares with your dog. The children would take turns playing. If you were an X you would lay down with your dog when called and if you were an O you would sit with your dog. You would play a round till it was a draw or somebody won. Beemer and I often signed up for that one.

Beemer Playing Tic Tac Toe with Misty

0	0	0
	O	X
	X	X

- Games and Contests – They would have all kinds of Obedience Games and Contests you could enter with your dogs. Best Costume, Kissing Booth, Relay Races, and Frisbee Competition to name a few.
- Gift Auction – they would have prizes you could buy tickets for to help raise money and possibly win a prize.
- Promote Adoption for Dogs - There was a booth set up promoting adoption for dogs from the shelters. The people running the booth even brought a few of the dogs that were available to be adopted. I would

love to adopt them all and rescue them like Beemer but for now Beemer was just settling in so it is something to consider for the future.

It is so important to promote adoption from the shelters. There are so many wonderful loving pets available. It was great that the school we took Beemer to actually volunteered their time to help train pets from the shelter so they would have a better chance at being adopted.

Beemer is a perfect example of a wonderful rescue. He knew what it was like to live on the street injured and alone. He knew what it was like to live behind a metal gate in the shelter for 6 months. Once Beemer was rescued from the shelter he loved life. He grew up and became a Certified Therapy Dog.

We found out that statistics show black dogs and cats are adopted less often than others. We were grateful Beemer was no longer included in those statistics. Who doesn't smile when they see a cute dog or cat. There are numerous TV shows of them doing something funny. The Puppy Super Bowl is a classic. The puppies featured are from shelters. They even added puppies and kittens in the view of the Yule Log at Christmastime.

On all our excursions whether pet visits or park walks whenever anyone said they wanted to get a pet we encouraged adopting from the shelter. We would say "They are the best. They always know they have a good home." "That's right." others would agree or say "I agree." We really try to help other animals like Beemer to find a good home as well as help people live better and healthier lives with pets.

Everyone benefits as they all have a purpose and days filled with love and laughter.

- Vendors – they would have many vendors come both dog and some not dog related. Massage, Reiki, Portraits, Dog items and Treats, etc.

- <u>Dog Walk</u>

    When you were ready to do the actual Dog Walk – at registration they handed out a map so depending on your dog you could do the short or long walk around the park. There were water and treat stations set up all around as you walked. We always brought our own but it was great that they had that available.

    After enjoying all the festivities we headed out on our walk. We took the short route since Mugsy was small and not used to walking as far as we did with Beemer. Towards the end of our walk poor Mugsy was getting hot and tired. Pugs can be prone to getting overheated. Kerri had to carry Mugsy for the last stretch.

    "Jack or I can carry him." I said to Kerri.

    "No I am good I can do it. I will let you know if it is too much."

    We made it back no problem and decided to call it a day. Both Beemer and Mugsy took a big drink and we blasted the AC for everyone in the car on the way home.

Beemer and Mugsy after the Dog Walk

We all had a great time. After that we decided to go every year.

The next year we went, Kerri did not come with us as she was busy with her new baby girl Lizzy. As we drove up we saw Katie in a Dalmatian costume with Misty. They looked absolutely adorable together. They were collecting for the Coin Toss.

Jack rolled down the window. "Hey we know you. Hi Misty."

Katie laughed. "Hi yes." She looked in the window. "Hi Beemer." Beemer was looking out wagging his tail a mile a minute.

"Hi how are you?" I said.

"Doing great. This is so much fun."

Jack tossed in money in her bucket.

"Thank you."

Since there were cars waiting behind us I said. "We'll come see you later. Have fun."

"Great. We will be here."

"Hey Beem you are going to see your friend Misty." Beemer was pacing back and forth in the backseat of the car. He could not wait to get out and explore. "Katie and Misty looked awesome. She is such a sweet person." I said to Jack.

"Yes she really is great." Jack agreed.

Every year we went they added more events and activities. They advertised it was fun for the whole family even if you did not have a dog. They had face painting and other activities for kids, Tricky Tray where you bought tickets and put in your ticket next to the prize you were interested in, Auction for Prizes and Contests.

Some of the Dog Contests:

- Fastest Dog – It was a relay race which Beemer won that year.
- Cutest Dog
- Best Costume
- Best Kisser

One year we even saw Beemer's Doctors there with their girls. A very fun event for a really great cause. We looked forward to it every year.

Beemer on the Dog Walk for Cancer

We also went to the local Baseball Stadium for the "Bark in the Park" events. Every year at the beginning of baseball season they would have a "Bark in the Park" day where you could bring your dog to the stadium. They also helped to promote Pet Adoption. We went with Beemer. It was fun plus Beemer got to enjoy a "Hot Dog."

Beemer's Tale 174

Beemer at 'Bark in the Park'

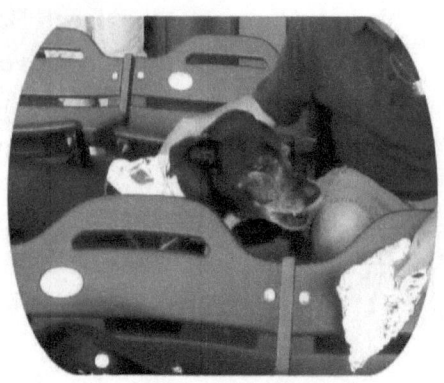

Lesson

Another life lesson learned and confirmed with our visits with Beemer:

To concentrate on helping someone or something other than yourself can make all the difference. It refocuses you to not think about all your problems or what is wrong in the world. Helping others even if only to give them a smile for a moment is the best reward.

Chapter 12 – Allergies and Diet

In 2006 Beemer developed Allergies. We first started noticing he was rubbing his eye a lot and it would start to get a little red. Whenever we saw him we would stop him and lightly rub it for him. Then he started itching intensely and making red marks or hot spots as they are called. Again when we saw him itching we would try to stop him and itch lightly for him. I would sing "Oooh oooh Itchyco I am going to itch you." As we were rubbing him his back foot would be moving as if itching along with us. Off to the Vet we went to have it checked out. We had him tested and he was allergic to several kinds of trees and grasses and he also had a chicken allergy. The Vet recommended limiting his diet and putting him on medication.

We also washed Beemer with Baby Oatmeal soap to help with itching and Gizzy's groomer Denise suggested to use V05 Hot Oil Treatment for conditioning. Beemer was so shiny and smelled so good like he went to the spa.

We put T shirts on him to help avoid licking and itching the spots so they could heal. Everyone would give us T shirts they wanted him to wear. I trimmed them so they would fit better on him. Beemer even got a T shirt with the Local Police Logo. That was one of his favorites as it was really soft. "Beemer you look so handsome!" we would tell him. Everyone would get such a kick out of seeing Beemer wear the T-shirt they gave him. One time we even had Beemer and Jack wear matching Tie-Dyed T shirts. Also with Beemer wearing a T-shirt we could still go on our Therapy visits. The people on our visits enjoyed seeing Beemer in his T-shirts.

Beemer in his T-Shirts

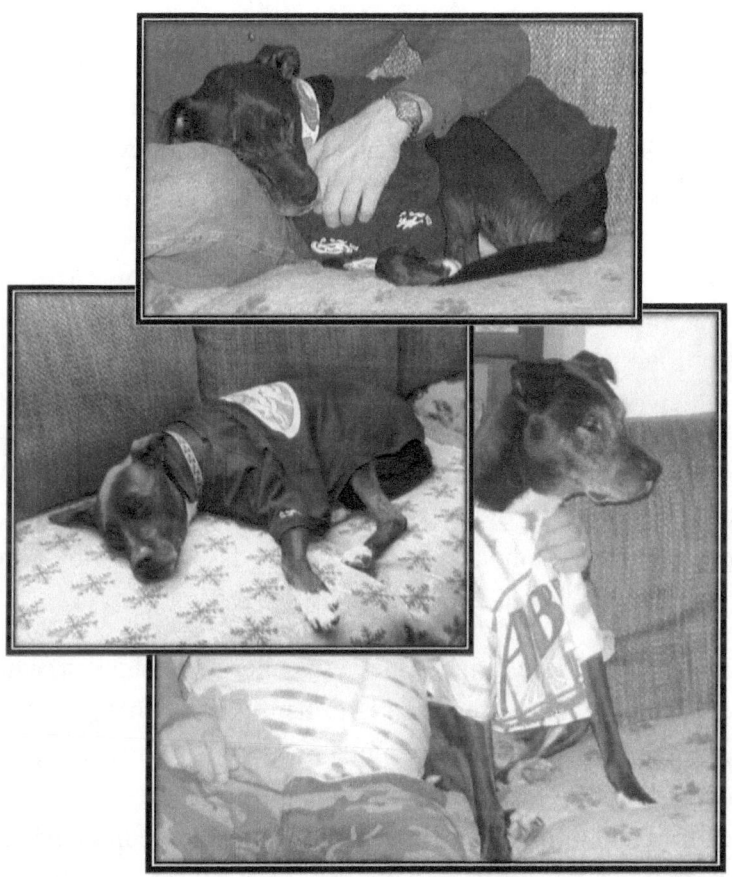

We decided to put Agility on hold for awhile so it would not aggravate his condition. Once on medication for awhile, Beemer's hot spots cleared up and he did not itch so intensely. He was good to go. We did go back to Agility on occasion but then we got so busy with Therapy Visits we put Agility on the back burner. We did make sure Beemer always got enough exercise to make up for it. During the week I would so look forward to taking Beemer to the park, especially after sitting in an office behind a computer all day. I would race home after work to

take Beemer when the weather was good and if it was Day Light Savings time. I would go in the bedroom to change and Beemer knew once I put my sneakers on. He flew out of the bedroom and waited at the door. If I was going to be late or if it was dark out then Jack would take Beemer during the afternoon. There is nothing better than getting outside for some fresh air and a walk. Beemer is a big fan and it makes Jack and I feel better too.

On weekends we would go twice a day. After breakfast Beemer would be waiting to go and could never settle down until we took him. Once we did he would lay down and relax and have a snooze once back home. Later in the day before dinner we would take him again and he was always ready to go.

Diet is so important. Since Beemer is allergic to chicken, which is a very common ingredient in so many kinds of dog food and treats, the Vet suggested we put him on an isolated diet. We tried Fish and Potato. He loved it which was great. We could add little additions like a little beef but it was recommended to minimize the options to help his condition. We believe that this diet had a lot to do with his overall health. His coat was always shiny and soft. He was getting lots of Omega-3 from his food. Since it was lean this also helped Beemer stay in great shape. We also give him filtered or bottled water.

We told all our friends "Jack made grilled or bronzed Salmon for dinner for Beemer to add to his food and we had hot dogs!" And that was ok since it is for our Beemer.

Another benefit was that Beemer never had a "dog" smell. His hair was very short and he always smelled great. We really feel that diet attributed to his overall condition.

One piece of advice from a valuable lesson we learned – spend the extra few dollars for your beloved four-legged ones and get them good quality food. It will be worth every penny in the long run.

Chapter 13 – Crossing Over

In September of 2005 we lost our dear Gerry. We are eternally grateful to her for giving us the opportunity to live in her house. It was similar in size to ours. We made plans to fix and expand the house in 2006. I made a rough sketch of what we thought we wanted and gave it to the Architect. We made a large kitchen, which Gerry would have loved and added a Master Bedroom and Bathroom. In June of 2007 we were able to move across the street to Gerry's newly constructed three bedroom house. We always call it Gerry's house out of respect and to honor her memory.

It was great for Beemer as he still had the familiarity of the same neighborhood and being close to all the parks. Plus we loved all our neighbors and friends who lived close by and did not want to leave the block.

Initially we were concerned Beemer would want to run across the street to go to his old house. He never did. He continued to follow the "No street without a leash" rule. We were amazed. He could have easily went there to smell and sniff where he used to live, but he never went unless we brought him there. Plus Beemer was already familiar with this place from visiting Gerry so often.

Life in Gerry's house is grand. We think Beemer loves his new house and new yard. There is more room, a better window view from the couch and for all of us a bigger bed. We had room for a Queen sized Bed – Heaven.

Beemer in his New Queen Bed

Beemer looking at his New Yard

Beemer's Tale 182

Beemer became a fixture on the front lawn; he is like a Lawn Statue or the Sphinx I thought. Beemer would lay on the front lawn in the shade under the Dog Wood tree. Beemer never left the property. Countless people would walk by, kids and adults commenting as they passed by. We got a lot of extra traffic as our street leads directly to the Dairy Queen on the corner.

"Hello. He looks so relaxed. He is so good."

Many kids on bikes would talk to Beemer as they rode by.

"Hey Beemer." April who lived down the street would say as she rode by our house with her friends or if we saw her on our walks. One time we heard April's friend said "Is that Beemer? The one you told us about? "

"Hi Beemer." Lizzy, Kerri's daughter, always said hello to Beemer as she rode by the house and Beemer was out.

Other children we never saw before would ride down the street on their way to Dairy Queen.

"Hi doggie."

"You are so cute!"

"Hey good doggie."

"Have a great day doggie."

"You are beautiful doggie."

The adults even commented as they walked by.

"Oh wow look at him – he is so well behaved."

"Hi. He looks so relaxed. He is so good."

"He is adorable. I can't believe he is just sitting there."

"OMG I didn't even realize he was there. He is so cute and he is so well trained."

Even our friend Lenny would yell from Sam's house "Beemer – I will be right over."

People could not believe he would just hang out and stay there even if another dog came by. He would stay and just wag his tail unless we said it was okay for him to get up to say hi. Then we would hook him up on his leash to let him see the other dogs. Beemer was so happy to be laying there unrestricted and watch everyone going by.

Beemer Hanging Out On the Lawn

Beemer's Tale 184

Our second bathroom in the new house had a walk in shower. We thought it would be perfect for giving Beemer a bath when it was too cold outside. The first time was great. We brought him in and we had a wand so we could let him step in and then wash him off. The next time it was time for a bath Beemer was laying on the couch. "Hey Beem. It's bath time." He knew what that meant. He sat up and put his head down. He jumped off the couch and walked slowly all the way down the hall to the back bathroom. Jack and I looked at each other.

"OMG I can't believe it. He is going on his own!" I said.

"He looks like he is walking the plank." Jack replied.

We followed him. Beemer walked right in the bathroom and waited at the entrance to the shower. "Aww Beem you are such a good boy. We will make it quick and then you get lots of treats."

"Good boy Beem." Jack added.

It was amazing. After that every time we said "It's bath time." Beemer would do his long slow walk down to the shower. "We really should video this because no one will believe us." I said.

"Yes we should." Jack agreed.

Beem Relaxing after his Shower

We joked and said Beemer has a couch in every room and wherever he went. We bought a new couch and moved our old couch in the garage until garbage day. When Beemer went outside he immediately went over to sniff the couch as it was new there and not supposed to be there. He immediately jumped on it and made himself comfortable looking out the front garage door. We laughed and I said to Jack "We can't throw this out now. He loves it." So Beemer even had a couch in the garage!

Beemer's Garage Couch

It may sound confusing to say front garage door. To clarify we have dual garage doors. One in the front and one leading out the back to the yard. Jack's Aunt's house had that set up when he was younger and lived with them. He thought it was the coolest and when we had this house built we decided to do the same here. There was really no other way to get machines or anything else needed in the yard other than to lift it over the fence. Everyone walking by looked when we had both doors open. Some even did a double take. We got many comments on how special it is. We love it as even if it is raining in the summer we can still have a barbeque as we do not park the cars in the garage. We have a long table and chairs set up and a stereo like we did across the street. It is the indoor/outdoor party room. Beemer loves that he can go freely from the backyard to the front yard.

Beemer in the Garage with Dual Doors

Shortly after moving, since Jack's Dad had passed and their dog Daisy had passed too, we moved Jack's Grandmother and Mother to our old house across the street. After discussion with Jack's brother we thought it was best to move them here. It was too far for us or his brother to be three hours away in case anything happened. Also his Mother did not drive so she had to rely on friends and family nearby to take her to the store and to

Beemer's Tale 188

doctor appointments. We had plenty of room in the new house so his brother and wife and the kids could come anytime to stay and visit. Beemer now had his PA friend Pepi to visit and play with on a regular basis.

Beemer and Pepi

Chapter 14 – Weather

Ever since Beemer came to live with us he was always impacted by the weather. We would open the door for him to go out and he would stand at the door and sniff the air before deciding if he wanted to go out. "Come on Beem. Are you going out or staying in?" Sometimes we would give him a little nudge to get him to step outside.

Beemer loves the sun. On sunny days it was no problem for him to go out. He would stand or lay out in the grass for as long as we would let him. Every day I would say "That's it – get your Vitamin D my boy."

We had to be careful on very hot days in the summer since he was black he would get hot very quickly. Over the years from laying in the sun so much he got brown highlights and was not as black all over as when he was younger. Whenever I would hug him I would smell him and say "Beemer you smell like you are Kissed by the Sun." And he did. He is our 'Sunbeem' every day. Beemer never has that dog smell even when coming in from the rain. We feel it had a lot to do with his sunbathing and diet. And of course regular showers and baths didn't hurt.

Beemer Kissed by the Sun

When Beemer was younger he was not really affected by Thunderstorms. But as he got older he became nervous whenever it would Thunder. We would know it was coming as before you heard the first Boom, Beemer would lay down and sometimes shake and sometimes try to hide. We felt so bad. There was no consoling him. We tried everything from Thunder Coats to sitting by him to turning up the TV or radio. We even tried to distract him with steak. Nothing worked. It just had to pass. Beemer would never eat when it thundered until the storm was over so we had to plan around it and try to feed him before the Thunder or wait till afterward.

When Beemer was younger he loved the snow. We would put his coat on and he would come out with us to shovel. I would point to the ground and say "Diggy Diggy" and Beemer would start digging in the snow. He did it every time. That one we actually captured on video.

Beemer 'Diggy Diggy' in the Snow

Beemer's Tale 192

When Beemer got older the rain and snow were not as fun for him. Beemer is our weatherman. Just as people feel stiffer in damp weather we could always tell when it was going to rain by the way Beemer walked to the door and of course his special sniff of the air when we opened the door and for him to decide if he wanted to go out or not.

Rain

>If it was raining really heavy sometimes Beemer would look out the door, sniff the air and turn right around to head back to the couch. "Can't blame him." I would say to Jack. "I really wish there was another way. When we are millionaires we will build a room or covered outhouse that will be Beemer's bathroom."
>
>If Beemer looked like he really had to go out then we would put on his raincoat. It only covered his back and not his head. I would go out with him wearing my hooded raincoat and follow him with one of those big golf umbrellas. It would help his head from getting soaked. If he had to do his business and not just pee then he would be out there for awhile to walk around before he would go. I am sure if the neighbors were looking out the window they were laughing at us but 'so what' it was worth it to us as it helped Beemer keep dry.
>
>One time on one of our walks to the park it was sunny one minute and then suddenly the rain came out of nowhere. The park had no shelter and we were not that close to home. "Ready Beem? We have to make a run for it." We ran down the main street since it was shorter than going our usual back street route and got the store at the corner of our street. They had an overhang where we could stop and catch our breath before making the

last stretch home. Beemer did a big shake with the water spraying in every direction. My T shirt was plastered on. I was sure I would have to pry it off. We waited to see if the rain would slow down or stop. By the look of the grey clouds in the sky it did not look like it was stopping anytime soon. This is when I say I want to be a weather person. They did not even predict this. They can give any readout on the weather and whether right or wrong they still get paid. "What do you think Beem? Should we head home?" Sometimes I wish he could answer me. We waited another few minutes and then I looked at Beem and said "Let's go." We ran down our street and made it in the garage. Jack was waiting with the door open with towels. "Quick quick get him dry." Good thing it was warm out. Jack said "I didn't know where you guys were so I didn't know which direction to go in." "Yes I know sorry. I forgot to bring my damn cell phone so I couldn't call." From then on I made sure I had the phone even if we were only going around the block.

<u>Hurricane Irene</u>

When news of the storm broke my sister called. "You should come stay with us."

"Thanks so much but that is going to be hard with Beemer and Pepi and Jack's Mother. I think, I hope it will be ok."

My sister lived an hour north from us. Turns out that we had less damage than my sister and other friends further north. My sister had a finished basement and unfortunately their whole basement got flooded. They lost computers and flooring and furniture. We had some water in the basement but minor in comparison. We were able to use the shop vac to suck it up.

You see the stories on the news about how they rescue pets and the owners are so happy to be reunited with their pets. It always brings tears to my eyes. It made me think of how far or for how long we could carry Beemer if we were in that situation. We could take turns carrying him over our shoulders since he was only about 50 pounds, but still for how long.

Jack said "We need a boat. One of those flat bottom boats." I looked it up and it is called a 'Jon Boat'. They range in price but they are around 500 dollars.

"Yes we should definitely get one." I agreed. It would be worth every penny.

I can just imagine Jack at the back end and I would be in the front rowing down the street with Beemer sitting in the middle. It would be perfect since Beemer did not really like the water and would not be happy swimming for too long.

Hurricane Sandy

Jack was always stressed about storms and took precautions to set us up for the worst case scenario before the storm hit and also for his Mother and Pepi across the street. If things got bad she could come and stay with us but she wanted to stay in her own space. Jack set up the LED candles in every room so we did not have to worry about any fire issues or blowing out candles. He set them up in front of the mirrors in the bedrooms to help throw more light. He put lanterns and flashlights in every room. He changed/charged batteries for the portable radio and spare batteries for the flashlights. He set up the Kerosene heaters just in case.

When the storm finally came it was interesting as there was no Thunder so Beemer was not scared and didn't shake like he usually did with Thunder. We went to stay in the basement for a while. We had a finished basement with a TV, a couch and table and chairs. When we thought it was ok we actually slept in the front bedroom since it was furthest away from the direction of the wind and the trees in the back yard. Our master bedroom was in the back of the house and closer to the trees so we thought the front bedroom was definitely better in case any branches or hopefully not but if any trees fell.

Then the power went out. We lost power and were in the dark for 9 days. I said I now know what it was like to be a pioneer. We did not have a generator so we were living with candles for light and boiling water over the open flame on the gas stove.

It was so amazing how quiet it was without any power. Other than the occasional dog barking or car driving by you heard nothing. Very peaceful.

Beemer did so well adjusting. When he had to go out at night we took him out with a large flashlight and lantern since there were no streetlights. It was like in the old times. We would go to bed early since there was no power for TV. Nine days really seemed like such a long time. Our first purchase once the power was back on was a generator.

It was great how everyone came together and helped each other out. Sam had hot water and offered anyone who wanted to take a shower. I had to travel an hour south for my job at the time and they had power there. I offered to get anyone milk or food as needed on my way home. Everyone at my work was so kind. They even offered for all of us to stay with them. It was very touching. "Truly thank you so much but we think we are ok roughing it for now. Hopefully the power will be on soon."

We were extremely lucky as we had very little damage in comparison to so many who lost so much. It was definitely too close for comfort though with major damage and destruction only two blocks away down near the Dock.

When the storm was over Beemer and I walked down to the Dock. The flooding damage was so sad; it was everywhere. We passed by one house and the lady was walking out to her car. I said "Hello. How are you doing?"

"Okay I guess. I was just coming out for a pair of socks." I noticed that they had put many of their belongings in the car to help protect them from the flood. "Such a cute dog." She said.

Beemer walked over to her and wagged his tail. She bent down and hugged him. "Yes he is a good guy. He is actually a Therapy Dog." I said.

"Oh wow that is so good you do that."

"Thanks. Yes everyone really enjoys it." I said with a sympathetic smile "Try to have a good day."

"You too."

"C'mon Beem." As we walked away I felt so bad. It was like a sick feeling in your stomach as you want to help but really don't know what to do. "Thanks Beem. Think she really needed a hug today."

Personally we escaped the wrath of Sandy this time but we truly know what it is like for all those people and what they are going through. So many lost so much. Years prior Jack's Grandmother's house was destroyed by a flood and Jack's parents lost their home by a fire. The whole house burnt to the ground as the Fire Engines could not make it up the mountain in time. Luckily no one was hurt. Jack's Dad was not home at the time and his Mom got out safely but had a few small burns trying to get Pepi out.

We could not bring Beemer with us when we went to help Jack's parents as we did not know where we would be staying. Our friend Sam said "Don't worry I will take care of Beemer. It will be a pleasure." We were so grateful.

We went and had to set his parents up in a hotel for a few weeks until they could get an apartment. It really makes you realize what is important.

Everyone agreed the hardest part whether by fire or flood is losing all the pictures, photographs, and heirlooms handed down over the years, a piece of jewelry or a special vase. These represented Memories and could never be replaced. Back then people did not have all their pictures on their phone or Facebook.

When things like that happen you gain a different perspective. It is not clothes and shoes and possessions that are important. It is the people and loved ones that are most valued. For us especially Beemer who could never be replaced.

Chapter 15 – Fun with Beemer

All the fun things you do with your pets where you can't help but smile and laugh with them and feel better.

We would take the tube from the wrapping paper or foil when it was done and walk slowly toward Beemer. Then we either said his name "Beemer" or made a horn sound "Dut do do". Beemer would get the 'crazies' as we called it running around the house like a nut in all directions. Our stomachs ached from laughing so hard.

We would play Frisbee with Beemer but of course as soon as he got it the game changed to chase Beemer to get the Frisbee back. It was always a good time. Whenever we had company with children, all the kids loved that one.

Chasing Beemer with the Frisbee

Beemer's Tale 200

Sometimes in the morning when Beemer woke up before us he would come over and sniff really loud in your ear "Ffft Ffft Ffft Ffft". It was cold and wet and tickled; it always makes us laugh. Beemer was never really a face kisser. On occasion he would kiss us if we asked but we taught him for our visits that if you held out your hand and said "Give kisses Beemer." He would kiss your hand just like a gentleman back in the day.

We even took Beemer to get his picture taken with Santa. We would display it every year at Christmastime.

Beemer *with Santa*

When Justin Bieber first became popular around 2009 I got an idea. Whenever we would take Beemer for walks and children came up to us they would ask "Can we pet your dog? What is his name?"

"His name is Beemer – just like Justin Beemer."

"Oooooh we love him!" All the little girls would squeal.

<u>Beemer's Birthday</u>

Happy Birthday Beemer!!!

Every year we celebrated Beemer's Birthday. We picked Halloween. Since Beemer was a rescue they could only estimate his age. We thought it would be fun as there would be visitors and activity all day. Beemer would get a special steak dinner. After the trick or treaters were gone we put a candle in a cup of vanilla ice cream, one of Beemer's favorites, and we would sing Happy Birthday. "Make a wish Beem." I would say and then blow out the candle. I took out the candle and let Beemer enjoy his Birthday Ice Cream.

Beemer's Tale

Happy Birthday Beemer!

After moving to Gerry's House we would always decorate the garage and leave the door open to have the Trick or Treaters come up the driveway for treats. Beemer would lay on his couch in the garage so he could see all the visitors for his Birthday.

The year we got his Superman costume for our Therapy Visits we dressed him up in it on Halloween. A set of kids started coming up the driveway and Beemer was excited. He hopped off the couch and started heading down the driveway with his tail wagging and his cape blowing in the breeze. One little boy must have been afraid of dogs and went running back toward his parents. I said "No it's okay he is friendly. He is a trained Therapy Dog." I assured the parents. The little boy was not convinced. I called Beemer to come back to the couch so the other kids could get their treats. I sent a handful of candy for the little boy with his sister so at least he got a treat.

After that we told Beemer to 'stay' when others came unless it was someone who knew him.

There was another group who came and this one little boy was dressed up like GI Joe; he was so adorable. The parents waited at the street and GI Joe came over with two friends.

"Trick or Treat!" they said.

"Happy Halloween! Take as many as you would like." I said as I held out the bowl.

"Thank You."

"You are very welcome."

Beemer stayed on the couch just watching. He was always so good. As they turned around they saw him and waved and said "Hi cute doggie."

"Today is Beemer's Birthday!" I said.

They smiled and waved to him. I wished them "Happy Halloween!" again as they headed down the driveway. All of a sudden GI Joe came running back up the driveway. He went right over to Beemer and kissed his head. "Happy Birthday Doggie" and ran back to his friends who were waiting with the parents at the edge of the driveway. That was such an "Awww" moment. "Thank you!" I said in return and waved as they left to go to the next house.

Beemer on Halloween

Beemer's Breed

As stated previously the number one question we always receive is "What kind of dog is he?"

On Beemer's adoption notice it said 'Lab/Pit Bull Mix.'

Facts about Labs:

Labrador Retrievers are one of the most popular breeds in the United States. They are famous for their love of the water as years ago they used to help fishermen.

They are Outgoing, Intelligent, Agile, Gentle, Kind and Trusting. Some people say they are not a good watchdog as they are so friendly they welcome everyone in your home. Their dedication to pleasing their owners makes them a reliable breed as a Therapy or Rescue Dog. They also have a very high pain threshold so it may be hard to know if something is bothering them.

Facts about Pit Bulls:

Pit Bull is not actually a breed but a term used to include formal breeds such as American Staffordshire Terrier, American Pit Bull Terrier and the Staffordshire Bull Terrier. They are Affectionate, Obedient, Loyal, Intelligent, Courageous, Friendly and Clownish.

Some say they are sweet, smart, hilarious and loyal companions. They excel at Agility for their strength and speed. Because of their people-pleasing nature they make excellent candidates for a Therapy Dog. They have an extreme tolerance for pain and often suffer in silence longer than other breeds. They can be prone to allergies.

Pit Bulls get a bad rap. Yes there are many bad stories and incidents that have occurred but that often has to do with upbringing, training, the owners and environment. Our experience has been the opposite. Beemer's Vet had a loving Pit Bull Molly who would come out and greet you and got along with everyone and the other dogs. Beemer is part pit and is the sweetest loving soul anyone has ever met.

Everyone has their opinion on what Beemer is. When Beemer ran he had the grace and speed of a Greyhound.

If he got excited when he would see another dog the hair would stand up straight down his back like a Ridgeback. When he played with our neighbor's dog, who was a Boxer; they swore Beemer was part Boxer. Beemer was tall and slim and had tiny narrow paws like a Pharaoh Hound. For insurance purposes we joked he could not be a Pit Bull so our vet said "He could be a Visala. No one ever questions about being a Visala."

Beemer was the perfect combination of both Lab and Pit Bull Mix. Beemer had the best qualities of each breed and any other type of breed he may also be mixed with.

Our final answer – Beemer is all the best of everything.

Beemer's Blog

It was a daily occurrence of compliments for Beemer from new people we would meet as well as people we came to know very well from going so often every time we were out. That was how I got the idea for 'Beemer's Blog'. The only time no one stopped us, which was rare, was if no one was in the park. To touch so many lives or even to get a smile for a moment was amazing. I was proud to be walking with Beemer.

Beemer's Blog is written from Beemer's point of view. We always felt Beemer had a human-like quality about him and how he could sense things. We were not the only ones who felt that way. Many others told us that as well. The idea was to share Beemer's stories of all the connections he made on our walks and Therapy visits. The goal is to help promote exercise, pet adoption from shelters, pet therapy and other topics of interest. I wrote ideas down but never found the time to actually get a site and post it. I wish I had as Beemer would have gone 'viral' as so many stories do today. Maybe I still will. It was fun when I wrote this first one. Always wished Beemer could talk like Goliath in 'Davy and Goliath' "Gee Davey" or Scooby Doo "Scooby Doobie Doooo!"

Here is an excerpt from

Beemer's Blog.

Hi! My name is Beemer and I live with Louann and Jack - they are my family. They don't say they are my Mom and Dad like I hear from some of my friends. We all go on a first name basis.

When I have to go to work to visit others in Assisted Living or Hospitals Louann is my handler.

My Topic of the Day – Allergies and Diet.

> *Can you believe I am allergic to all the things I love? Grass and trees. I know a lot of people are allergic to them too. I have to take medication to help with the sneezing and itching. If you think you have allergies too then you should check with your doctor. Louann and Jack took me and it definitely helps!*
>
> *Diet can also help. I started eating fish and it is really delicious you should try it. Something*

about Omega and the other good things it does for you.

Today's Adventure

Today we went to the Beach Park. One of my favorites. It is a park and a beach – Paradise! The parking lot was very crowded. There were a lot of people in the park. As we walked around, some young girls asked if they could pet me. I learned they were there for a picnic and they played in the High School Band. Cool. I love music. I met two of the clarinet players and one girl was from the Color Guard. They were so sweet. They each bent down and gave me a hug. Louann told them how I always where a bandana with the school colors when we go to the parades. "Go Panthers!" Louann said. I wagged my tail. "Awesome" was their reply.

We then continued our walk behind the Waterfront Condos. Wow to live in those. I could be at the Beach Park Every Day! Sweet! One can dream no? But for now just visiting. We met another member of the Band. His name was Aaron. He had thick blond curly hair. Aaron asked what I was and they told him I was part Lab and part Pit. He said how he was leery of Pit Bulls as he was bitten by one once on the leg. Pit, Schmidt – they get a bad rap. It is the owners who are .... Don't get me started - I digress. Anyway back to Aaron. He told us about his two Shelties and how his family was a Sheltie Foster Home where they try to find new homes for them. Now that is such a good thing.

A Foster home is so much more comfortable than the shelter. Take it from one who spent 6 months behind bars. We bid farewell to Aaron and continued with our walk.

What's that smell? "MMMMmmm" My nose is high in the air enjoying the smell of grilling on fresh charcoal wafting our way. I made a mad dash toward the Picnic area only for my leash to get a slight tug indicating I was not invited to the Picnic. Bummer. But then I was told we were heading to the store to get some things for our own Picnic/Dinner. Ahh – I love September! Weather is still nice and cool and you can still Grill!

Until next time - Keep Walk'in!

At the next Parade where the High School Band played we saw Aaron in the lineup. He spotted us on the sideline and Jack and I waved and I pointed to Beemer who was wearing his gold bandana. Jack and I joked Beemer could be their mascot. Aaron remembered us or I should say he remembered Beemer and he smiled and nodded.

Beemer's Buddies

Beemer made so many friends over the years not just in the people world but in the animal world. Pets of Friends, Family, Neighbors and people we met from school and on our way to the park and in the park that we would see often.

Beemer's Tale

We would not have met so many wonderful people and animals if it was not for Beemer.

Here are some highlights of Beemer's Buddies.

Gizmo

Gizmo was Beemer's girlfriend. We called her Gizzy for short. Beemer loved Gizzy. She was a sweet Lhasa Apsa – white with brown patches. They always got along great. They would lay on the couch together and love to hang out in the yards together. Gizmo was 10 years his senior.

Our one friend Lenny, who is a musician, even wrote a song about Gizmo and her friend Beemer.

One of Beemer's jobs was to go over with Jack to feed and let Gizmo out whenever Sam would go away or was coming home late from work.

When Gizmo got older she lost her hearing and eyesight. It was so sweet to watch whenever Beemer and Gizmo were together, Beemer would help guide Gizmo in the house or in the backyard so she would not bump into things.

It was a very sad day when Gizmo passed for everyone who knew her. One of Gizmo's favorite spots was to lay in the corner of her backyard in the shade under the oak tree. Every time Beemer goes in Sam's yard since she passed he still goes over to that very spot first thing as if remembering Gizmo.

Misty

Misty is a sweet Dalmatian and Beemer's first friend at school. Misty belongs to Katie who we became friends with when we all attended training together. Beemer really enjoys every time we would see Katie and Misty at the park near our house or sometimes at Summerfest.

"How are the visits going?" Katie asked.

"Great. We have been going to Assisted Living Facilities and Home Visits for friends who cannot get out. I see besides Assisted Living you guys go to "Reading with Dogs" at the Library for the kids."

"Yes. Yes we do. All the children love it. It is such a good program."

"Yes we always see your picture in the paper – Awesome. I wish we could do that one but since it is during the day unfortunately we cannot go because of my work."

"Yes that is a shame since Beemer is such a sweetie."

"Well if you hear of any other places we can do nights and weekends."

"Sure will definitely keep that in mind."

"So great to see you."

"You too."

We hugged and I pet Misty and Katie pet Beemer.

"Bye Misty."

"Bye Beemer."

Layla

Layla is a sweet shepherd mix with white and brown spots. We often saw her with her owner as we both walked every day it was nice. We would be walking in opposite directions so we were walking towards each other. The first time we met, her owner explained "Layla is kind of submissive."

"That's okay. Beemer is friendly to everyone."

Layla layed down and showed her belly to Beemer.

"Aww that is so cute." I said. "I think they are friends already."

"Yes definitely." Beemer went over and sniffed and wagged his tail. Then Layla got up and gave Beemer a sniff.

"Have a good walk."

"You too." And we were all on our way. That became our routine every time we saw them.

Tweed

Tweed is the cutest little miniature poodle. Tan in color and was always so happy to see people. She is a little shy of bigger dogs since she is so tiny. Who could blame her. After a few meetings with Beemer, Tweed welcomed Beemer and they became friends. Tweed would always come over to greet me first. Then Beemer and Tweed would do the dance of tangling leashes to get a sniff and say hello in their own way. In our conversations with Tweed's Mom, we found out they moved down here to retire. They used to live in my hometown where I grew up.

Beemer's Tale 214

Bandit

Bandit is a tan and brown Labradoodle who lived in the house directly across the street from the entrance to the Bird Sanctuary. We often ran into them on our walks there. "There's your friend Bandit Beem." Bandit is a little taller than Beemer. They wagged and said hello. Always happy to see each other.

Lucy

Lucy lived directly behind us. We could peek through the fence to see her. Lucy is a black wire haired terrier mix. She reminded me of a bigger version of Toto from the 'Wizard of Oz.' We became friends with her owners or parents as some people say - Natalie and Matt. Whenever Lucy came out and Beemer was in the yard, Lucy would run up to the fence barking at Beemer. Beemer never responded with barking. He would just stand at the fence and sniff. They would go nose to nose through the fence. When we finally got to meet them face to face from walking around the corner Lucy was so friendly to Beemer without a bark. Guess it was the unknown from behind the fence. After meeting face to face Natalie and Matt invited us over whenever they had a party and of course Beemer was also invited.

When Natalie and Matt moved away, they did not move too far so sometimes we would see them on our walks. Natalie would stop and role the window down. "Beemer how are you doing?" Beemer would come up to the window but never jumped on the car.

"We are good thanks."

"How's the new place and how is Lucy? We miss you guys."

"Doing good. New place is coming along and Lucy is well. She is with my sister right now while I am doing errands."

"Good to see you. Give her a hug and kiss from us."

"Will do. Take care Beemer. You are such a good boy."

<u>Babe</u>

Babe is a handsome husky shepherd mix. He belongs to our neighbors, Sheila and Ben, right next door. Babe is very sweet. He has a beautiful coat which was white and brown. Babe has a widow's peak in brown that went around his eyes. We thought he looked like Eddie Munster from 'The Munster's' TV show.

Our neighbor's asked if we would feed and let Babe out when they went away to Atlantic City for the weekend. It was the perfect alternative to getting another dog. We just watched everyone else's while they were on vacation. This way Beemer got to play and it was only temporary. Beemer and Babe had fun together. They would play all day and Jack and I would take them on walks together. Then we would put Babe back in his own house at bedtime.

Pepi

Pepi was Jack's parent's dog. He is a cute tan fluffy Pomeranian. Beemer met Pepi first in Pennsylvania at Jack's parent's house. Then they became buddies when we moved Jack's Mom and Grandmother along with Pepi to live across the street in our old house. Pepi was a barker. Beemer just always looked around to see what Pepi was barking at.

When we had Jack's Grandmother and Mother over to our house with Pepi we would always put a ball out for Pepi to play with. Pepi did the cutest trick where he would put his front paws on top of the ball and walk it around like in a Dog Act. Once Pepi jumped down Beemer grabbed the ball and took off hoping Pepi would chase him.

Beemer's Tale 218

Jocco and Dante

Jocco is a tan Boxer. After we moved to Gerry's house across the street we had 'new next door neighbors' even though we already knew them. Beemer got to play with Jocco. The two of them would run together back and forth across the two lawns. Quite comical as Beemer always did his "Spin" and Jocco would get tired out much quicker than Beemer. We always put out a big bowl of water so side by side they would take a drink.

When Jack wanted Beemer to go outside right away and to not keep standing and sniffing out the door he would say "Go see Jocco." Beemer would fly out to see if Jocco was there. "Aww that's not fair." I would say to Jack. "Well it got him out and maybe Jocco is outside."

Jocco was another one we would watch when his family was on vacation. Jack would bring Beemer over to feed Jocco and then let the both of them play together. Jocco went back in his own house for bedtime.

A few years later they got a second dog; a new boxer puppy named Dante. He was adorable and Beemer and Dante would run around but as puppies do Dante would sometimes nip at Beemer. One time Beemer gently put his paw on Dante as to say "That's enough."

<u>Xena</u>

Xena is an adorable black and white Shih Tzu. We called her Xena Warrior Princess. Xena belonged to Helen who lived three doors down from us. Helen was one of the seniors who still lived on the block which I knew from when I was young. My sister and I used to play with Helen's children when we came to visit our Grandparents. Now that her children were older and had moved away Helen got a dog to keep her company.

"She keeps me walking but more like pulling me down the street. You can't believe how strong she is." We could see Xena was strong for Helen and definitely needed some obedience training. Every time Helen would see Beemer and he would come over to see her and Xena, Helen would say "He is so handsome and sleek. Such a good dog. Not like this one."

"Oh Xena is so cute."

"Yes but not trained like Beemer."

"Just takes a little practice."

"I'm too old."

"No you are never too old."

When Beemer and I would walk by Helen and Xena's house Xena would run back and forth across the windowsill and the curtains would go flying. I would pick up the pace to go by faster, "Let's go Beem before the curtains fall down."

It was great for Helen to have the motivation to get out and walk with Xena. They both benefited from the exercise and socialization to see and speak to others.

Rusty, Buddy and Pepper

Rusty, Buddy and Pepper are my sister's dogs. Beemer first became friends with Rusty, a sweet Shepherd mix, who was older than Beemer. They had great respect for each other.

Then they got Buddy, a mix of Burmese Mountain Dog and Rottweiler, so Mikey would have a younger dog to play with. Buddy would learn from Rusty and they got along well together. Rusty was so patient especially having a new puppy on his tail. On holidays and visits Beemer loved to see them every time we all got together either at our house or hers. It was very sad when Rusty passed. He truly was a very sweet guy and loved Mikey and was always there for him. We often watched Buddy when my sister, her husband and Mikey went on vacation. I would walk Buddy and Jack would walk Beemer. We joked Buddy was going on vacation at the shore. Initially Buddy was dominant and was a powerhouse. He would almost knock Beemer down to get out the door first. Eventually Buddy adapted and Beemer and Buddy became friends.

After awhile so Buddy would have a companion after Rusty passed they got Miss Pepper. Mikey wanted another dog and he saw Pepper online. Pepper is a little Jack Russell/Daschund mix. She is very cute and loves to sit on your lap. All three Beemer, Buddy and Pepper run around the yard like crazy whenever they get together.

Jack the Cat

When Sam got married his wife Ami had a cat named Jack. He was orange and reminded me of Garfield. Ami said "He loves to eat." Yes definitely Garfield I thought. Beemer and my Jack would always go to take care of 'Jack the Cat' when Sam and Ami went away. Jack is allergic to cats. If he pets them then he has to wash his hands right away otherwise if he touches his eyes they will get swollen. If he gets scratched then the scratch will also become swollen. Funny how cats are attracted to Jack and go right over to him. Beemer would walk in and Jack the Cat would come over and lay down and show his belly to Beemer. It was so sweet. They would sniff each other and Jack would then follow Beemer around the house.

On several occasions when we were all hanging out in Sam's yard they would let Jack the Cat out. Beemer and Jack would greet each other nose to nose. They truly liked each other. It was definitely a Kodak moment.

Fluffy

Fluffy is a cute white fluffy dog – just like her name. I remember the first time we met Fluffy and her owner

Dawn. We were on our way to the Dock and this lady was walking with a little white fluffy dog.

"Hello. He is handsome who is this?" she said to us as we got closer. I smiled.

"Hi. This is Beemer. And what is your puppy's name?" I called all dogs no matter how old puppies.

"This is my Fluffy."

"Aww she is so cute."

"Beemer is very friendly." She bent down to pet him.

"Hello Beemer. You are such a good boy aren't you?"

"Yes he is. He loves all animals as you can see. And he is a Therapy Dog." Beemer was wagging his tail and sniffing Fluffy.

"Oh how wonderful. Fluffy is very friendly too and so am I."

I laughed. "My name is Louann. Nice to meet you both."

"I am Dawn."

"We are on our way down to the Dock. We walk here all the time."

"We will look for you and definitely see you again."

"Great. Have a good day. Bye Fluffy."

"You too. Bye."

As we continued on our walk I said "See Beem you made a new friend." Funny how different they were here Fluffy was small and white and Beemer was tall and black.

The next time we saw Dawn she was walking two different dogs. "Hi how are you? Where's Fluffy? And who are these two cuties?" I said. One was a brown hound mix and the other was a small terrier mix.

"Fluffy's at home. I am walking these two. The brown one is Jake and the small one is Lady."

"Aww they are so cute."

"I actually am starting to offer a dog walking service. I was doing it for many of my friends and said why not do it full time."

"Good for you."

"I get to exercise and do something I love AND get paid for it."

"Nothing better than that. I will keep that in mind in case I know anyone who may need your service."

"Excellent – I am having cards made up so will give you one next time."

"Great thanks."

Daisy and Dudley

On our walks to the Dock and the Sanctuary there was this corner house with a fenced in yard. We often would see a brindle pit mix. She was very cute. She would run back and forth the length of the fence as we walked by. Beemer would go up to the fence and she would just want to run back and forth and then would jump up with her paws on the fence and I would pet her. One time her owner was out and she said "Hi I am Kasey and this is Daisy."

"Hi Daisy. This is Beemer and I am Louann. We live on the next street over."

"I see you going by. We walk down your street sometimes."

"Well if we are out stop by anytime so Daisy and Beemer can see each other."

"Great thanks."

And so Beemer had another new buddy. We would walk by and see "Crazy Daisy" as we called her as she got the crazies running back and forth whenever she saw Beemer. Sometimes we saw Kasey and Daisy walk by and they would stop so Daisy and Beemer could see each other. Daisy was not so crazy on the leash.

A few years later Kasey got another dog. A black and white pit mix. Dudley is solid muscle and strong. "Who is this cute guy?" I said as Kasey was coming up the driveway.

"This is Dudley. I got him to keep Daisy company while I am at work."

"Aww he is really cute." "

He is sweet too like Beemer. Daisy and Dudley love running around in the yard together."

"Yes Daisy definitely loves to run."

After they left "See Beem you made another new friend today."

Kasey would take turns walking either Daisy or Dudley and we would see them as they passed by. If we went by Kasey's house and they were out Beemer would get to see both Daisy and Dudley.

<u>Winston</u>

Winston is a little black pug who is so energetic and cute. Winston belongs to Annie and Don; they are Kerri and Colin's neighbors. They walk Winston down the street every day that it is nice out.

The first time they came by and Beemer was out Winston came right over. Winston and Beemer would run around our front lawn together. So fun to watch them run and play. Winston is so tiny. Beemer always had a sense for puppies and smaller dogs. Beemer is always careful to take in consideration their size.

Ever since that first day every time Annie and Don would walk Winston, Winston always started coming up the driveway looking for Beemer even if he wasn't outside. It is so sweet. Winston is so friendly and gives kisses. When we were out they would play together and Annie always said "Beemer you just made Winston's day!"

Jack calls him his 'Winstagram.'

Ruby

Ruby is a tan dingo from Puerto Rico. She belongs to another neighbor further down the block. Ruby is very sweet and shy. We told David she just needs to be socialized and she will get better. She is always receptive to Beemer as he is so calm whenever they would see each other.

David is so thoughtful. He brings us marrow bones for Beemer.

Hunter

Hunter is a tan and black shepherd mix who is also a rescue from the shelter. Hunter belongs to Paul and Diana who live across the street from Sam. Hunter is very sweet. Paul and Diana have a swimming pool in their back yard so they always bring Hunter out to their front yard to do her business or they take her on walks.

Whenever Beemer and I would walk by and Hunter was outside, Hunter and Beemer would say hello. They got along great. If they walked by our house and Beemer was out, Beemer would go to the edge of the lawn to see Hunter. If Hunter was inside looking out the window she would always bark. I would say "Hi Hunter" and wave as we passed by. "Hopefully Hunter will be out next time Beem."

<u>Willow</u>

Willow is black and white. Willow lives on the next block. We first noticed her behind the fence as she looked a little like Beemer. She did not have the white feet like Beemer, but she was black with white on her chest. Also her ears were a lot longer which reminded us of a hound dog. We guessed she was maybe Lab mixed with some kind of hound. They have a corner lot and the fence ran along the side of their house and around the front. One day we saw her owners outside and we stopped. "Hi we thought they look like they could be related. This is Beemer. What is her name?"

"Yes they do look alike. Her name is Willow."

"Hi Willow." I said and petted her over the fence.

"Beemer is very friendly. He is a rescue from the shelter and is a Therapy Dog."

"Really? That is great. We got Willow from the shelter too."

"They are definitely the best. I think they know they have a good home. She seems really sweet."

"Yes she is and she is great with our son. "

"That is awesome."

Willow was so happy every time we walked by. I would say "Hi Willow." And she would come right over to the edge of the fence. Beemer and Willow would sniff and wag tails. Then Willow would try to run. Since I had the long lead for Beemer the two of them would run back and forth the length of the fence on opposite sides.

Beemer truly loves all animals. He makes so many buddies and friends both people and animals on our travels and in the neighborhood.

Bulldog Rescue

A good friend of mine is the head of one of the NJ Bulldog Rescue Services in NJ. Karen works so hard to find the rescues medical care and new homes. She works and attends many fund raiser's including ones widely known and run by celebrities including Beth Stern, Howard Stern's wife, and Ice Tea and Coco. We tease her she is our only friend who has pictures on the 'Red Carpet.' I give her kudos and credit for all the hours she puts in to help others.

My friend Joe and I used to work with Karen. Every holiday Karen would dress her bulldog Zimmer up in costume and take a picture to send to everyone. "Aww he looks so cute." I would say.

Karen's organization runs many local fund raisers and events like the 'Beach Bash' where everyone gathers on the beach with their Bulldogs and have refreshments and enjoy the day. Another event is the 'Dog Social' at one of the local bars that have an outside patio so people can bring their Bulldogs to the event. Karen met Beemer at one of the Outside Summer Concerts we attended together. "He is so calm and sweet" she said. After that Beemer was invited to attend all the Bulldog events. It was an honor to be invited. Beemer could be inducted as an "Honorary Bulldog." So funny to think of Beemer being tall and thin amongst all the short and stout Bulldogs, but he loves all dogs so it is a perfect match.

Beemer's Best Time of Year

We believe Beemer's favorite time of year is the Fall. The weather is still nice and he loves to smell the leaves on the ground.

Beemer also likes Springtime too as after being cooped up all winter and the weather is finally getting better to go on longer walks.

I love the Summer but sometimes it is too hot for Beemer. Even though he loves the sun, we had to monitor so he did not stay in the sun too long and get overheated.

We decided fall was number one; maybe because his Birthday is in October but it is probably because of the leaves and the weather. Everyone in the neighborhood would rake their leaves and put them in big piles at the end of the lawn. They would stay there until the town came to pick them up. Beemer would stick his head way into the pile of leaves like an ostrich. He would poke his head back out and he would have pieces of leaves stuck all over his head. "Beem what did you do?" I would gently brush them off just in time before we moved to the next pile. Beemer also loves to stick his head far in the bushes and smell. "What are you doing in there? Something smell good?" When he went near the brush where there were thorns I had to pull to keep him away. Walks take so much longer in the Fall as he has to smell every pile as we pass by.

Fall – Beemer's Favorite Time of Year

Chapter 16– Daily Life – Part 2

Life changed when we moved to the new house in 2007. We had more room inside and outside and of course our bigger bed!

Once in the new house Beemer learned my work routine. It really wasn't that different from when we lived across the street, but because it was a new house there were some slight changes. I would get up, take a shower and get dressed. Sometimes Beemer would get out of bed for me to let him out before I left and sometimes he would sleep in with Jack. As always I went and hugged and kissed him and then blew him a kiss good bye. "Have a great day my beauty. I will see you later."

When it is bedtime I would say to Beemer "It's last call" as we went out for the last time that day to do business before going to bed. When we came in then we would go to bed and it was "Time to watch Jerry in Gerry's house." We would watch Jerry Seinfeld in bed together before lights out.

We had to find a new place to hang Beemer's portrait. We could not find the right place for it when we first moved in. It is now displayed on the mantle over our faux fire place. It is the perfect spot. We have an electric fireplace with a heater. It actually looks nice and without the mess of a real fire.

When it is time to go in the car some days Beemer was so excited he would leap off the back stairs. "OMG Beem easy does it." We never wanted him to get hurt. We put one of those thick rubber mats at the bottom of the stairs to help cushion his landing. We also put runners on the stairs to make them less slippery for wintertime.

When we moved it was time to get Beemer a new coat. His old coat needed to be replaced. His new one is a bright blue one. This one was a little longer so it covered his back end more. It is great for keeping him dry on those rainy days. We also got him a light weight one if it was a little chilly. It was purple and looked great on him. Everyone said he looked handsome.

Before we moved across the street it was great as Rob would come and stay with Beemer if we wanted to get away or go on vacation. As the years passed when Rob got remarried and was busy with his new family, either Sam or other family members would watch Beemer. We did not go away that often but when we did we knew Beemer was well taken care of in his own home. One time Jack's brother and his girlfriend came to our house to stay with Beemer. Since they lived upstate New York and love coming to the shore to stay with us for visits and vacation it worked out perfectly. We all got a vacation.

Beemer's Tale 236

Music to My Ears

Music is a big part of our lives. We have many friends who are musicians and just love music in general. We love all kinds of music. We always have music playing. Beemer does not like loud electric music. He prefers acoustic.

Beemer Enjoying our Friend Lenny Playing Acoustic

Jack is the like the house DJ and always plays songs for every occasion. At parties he gets requests from friends as he has a large music collection.

I love to sing and sing to Beemer all the time since day one. Not the whole song but a few lines at a time. I used to sing in chorus and in plays in high school. I would change the words to fit Beemer and sing songs depending on what was going on. I would sing tons of songs to Beemer but there were some common ones that I sang often. When I hit high soprano notes his ears would definitely be on radar.

Playlist

"Beautiful Boy" by John Lennon – sang this one a lot.

"Saturday Night's Alright" by Elton John – "It's Saturday Saturday Saturday Saturday..." every Saturday morning.

"Let's hear it for the Boy" by Deniece Williams – "Let's hear it for the Beem." – whenever he would so something that needed to be rewarded.

"Ooh Ooh Itchycoo - I am going to Itch You" think I made it up but kind of like the tune of "Witchy Woman" by the Eagles - whenever he had an allergy itch. I would rub his itchy spot and he would wiggle his back end or his paw would go back and forth while I was rubbing his itchy spot.

"Shake it Off " by Taylor Swift - "Shake it Off like Taylor Swift" for allergies and whenever something was bothering him.

I would hum a marching band tune in the house when getting ready to go on our walk. Beemer would wag his tail to the music heading to the door. Beemer was like a Maestro with his tail.

"Zip-a-Dee-Doo-Dah" sung by James Baskett/Uncle Remus from the Walt Disney movie 'Song of the South'- when we were in the park and Beemer was smelling something too long I would start singing and he would start to walk and pick up the pace.

"Mr. Lee" by the Bobbettes - "Mr. B Mr. B Oh Mr. B" whenever the mood struck.

"Stayin Alive" by the BeeGees – "Oh Oh Oh Oh Stayin Alive Staying Alive" whenever Beemer did is John Travolta pose.

"Oh What a Beautiful Morning" by Gordon MacRae from Oklahoma – sometimes when we would wake up in the morning.

"Good Morning" from the movie 'Singin' in the Rain'– "Good morning Good morning oh what a lovely day let's go out and play Good morning" when we would wake up and know it was a park day.

"Beautiful Day" by U2 – "It's a beautiful day, don't let it get away, It's a beautiful day." when it was nice out and we were definitely going to the park.

"Nothin' on You" featuring Bruno Mars - "They got nothin' on you Beemer, Nothin' on you Beemer " - when he got a compliment.

"Just the Way You Are" by Bruno Mars - "Boy you are amazing just the way you are" whenever he made me smile.

"Treasure" by Bruno Mars – "Treasure, that is what you are, Beemer you're my golden star" - anytime it fit.

Can you tell I love Bruno Mars?

"Sugar Bee, Sugar Bee" written by Eddie Shuler – "Sugar Bee, Sugar Bee, Oh Sugar Bee" whenever we would have dessert.

"Romeo's Tune" by Steve Forbert – "Meet me in the middle of the night and let me see that everything's alright" sometimes when we were going to bed.

"Everything is Awesome" by Tegan and Sara from the Lego Movie - when doing our laps inside the house.

"This is How We Do It" by Montell Jordan – when doing our laps.

"Exercise, exercise come on everybody do your exercise!" by Bob McAllister from Wonderama – also when doing our laps.

One of my friends is a big Barry Manilow fan. So Beemer's song from his play list is… "The Miracle is you. You are a true blue spectacle - the miracle is You … Woo." And I would point at Beemer. Think Beemer gave me the look like I was nuts on that one.

Jack always said – Living with Beemer is 'Like a Peaceful Easy Feeling' by the Eagles.

"Whatever was going on Beemer is a staple and never a problem or a hassle. Beemer helps us through life and enhances our life."

<u>Calming Music</u>

Originally Beemer was timid and shy of large boxes and bags from the grocery and even the vacuum cleaner. He would jump off the couch until the coast was clear. One time our musician friend Lenny came over before one of his shows in the area to rehearse before the show. Beemer was laying on the couch and Lenny and one of the other musicians who would be performing at the show with him walked in. They brought in Guitar Cases and a Cello with Music Stands. They set up and started to play. We had hard wood floors so it was louder than if we had carpet and echoed in the living room. It sounded wonderful. Jack was sure Beemer would disappear to one of the bedrooms. Jack walked in and saw Beemer relaxing to the music. Jack was amazed Beemer was hanging out on the couch enjoying the show before the show. We could not believe Beemer stayed the whole time just listening to the music.

At one of our walks at the Beach Park we saw a young boy playing his guitar and singing on one of the picnic tables. Beemer was wearing his purple coat which was a lightweight coat and not as heavy as his winter/raincoat. We called it Beemer's Easter coat since it was purple. The boy looked up and saw us. He started strumming his guitar harder and sang "Doggie in the Purple Coat,

Purple Coat. Doggie in the Purple Coat." That was all we heard as we continued on our way. I turned to Jack and smiled "Hey you never know – he could be the next Prince singing about the Purple Coat instead of Purple Rain!"

Beemer in his Purple Coat

Take Your Child to Work Day

Many people often commented how Beemer was more like a person than a dog. I never really ever called him a dog. I always said "My four legged guy" as he was like my kid.

Every year on 'Take your Child to Work Day' my workplace would have a lots of events planned for the children. Since I did not have children of my own I would always volunteer to help out as a guide to walk the children through the building from event to event. I often entertained the idea of bringing in Beemer since he was a trained Therapy Dog. Beemer hardly ever barked so no one would even know he was there if he hung out in my office and the kids would have loved it. I never did as I thought after a few hours he would be bored especially since there was no couch in my office for him to lay on.

Other people have brought service dogs in training into work to get them used to the work environment.

I wish I had brought Beemer into work. After 28 years of service, my job was outsourced. I lost my pension and my job. It was very sad as I was one of the few people who could say I loved my job and loved going to work every day. I am very grateful for Beemer as he cheered me up and keeps me positive. Since I was home every day while looking for a new job we got to go on lots of extra walks. Beemer was happy as he thought every day was Saturday.

School Bus

Sam got married to his wife Ami in 2009. They had a daughter named Holly. When it was time for Sam's daughter to go to school for the first time Jack walked with Ami down the corner to meet Holly at the bus. All the kids love to see Beemer. "He is so cute." One of the other children said.

Holly introduced him. "This is Beemer and he visits patients. He lives across the street from my house and always comes over. He is a really good dog."

"Can he come back tomorrow?" one of the other kids asked Jack.

"Sure." Jack said. Beemer is a hit every day he is at the Bus Stop.

Tracker

The other thing that Beemer constantly did on a daily basis was to point out anything that was moved or changed in the house or outside. It was hilarious to see him go up and smell anything that was new or moved. We even did experiments and move things when he wasn't there to see if he would know. Each and every time he would go up to whatever the object was and smell. "There he goes again." Jack said and we would laugh.

"We should have sent him to training to be a tracker!" I would exclaim.

If it was a bag or a potted plant or even just a blanket we moved to a different side of the couch he would go up and smell it. I think he would have made a great drug sniffer or identifying people in wreckage or even maybe join 'Rosco' as a Bed Bug worker. He truly has the gift of smell.

Beemer's Gift of Smell

<u>Keep your chin up</u>

One night before bed I noticed Beemer's eye was running. I went and got a washcloth and ran it under warm water and walked over to him. "What's happening there my boy." He let me wipe his eye and hold the warm compress over his eye for a minute.

"Jack we are going to have to watch this."

"What?"

"Beemer's eye is running. My poor beauty."

The next morning when I opened my eyes as always I immediately look at Beemer to give him a morning hug and kiss. His back end is always toward me and his head towards the end of the bed. To my horror his face was so swollen and his eye was almost closed. He tried to yawn and let out a little cry in pain. "OMG." My eyes started to tear up and I darted up out of bed to see him face to face. Jack woke up abruptly. "What's the matter?" he said with alarm. "Look OMG my poor beauty. Don't worry we are going to fix this." I tried to gently pet him on his shoulder as to not touch anywhere near his face where he was swollen. The side of his face looked like a St. Bernard with his jowl hanging down. "I am calling the vet as soon as they open." I was so upset. Beemer got up and hopped off the bed. I followed him right out. He went to get a drink and the water poured out the side of his mouth that was swollen. "My God – this is so awful." I said aloud. I do not want to see him suffer in any way. I hoped and prayed to all the powers that be to help him.

We took him to the vet and his Doctor, Dr. M., was off that day and we had to see one of the covering doctors. She took one look and said "This looks like a tooth infection." She gave him a shot of Penicillin and sent us home with antibiotics. "It should clear up in a day or two." A day or two? I thought - OMG this has to clear up now! We had to feed him only soft foods like mashed potatoes so he could lick the food as he cried if he tried to chew anything.

By the grace of God and prayers to St. Frances the next morning the swelling started to come down.

Beemer's Doctor had suggested putting him under to clean his teeth but we were concerned about putting him under anesthesia. After he got the infection we wondered if that was the best decision not to do the teeth cleaning. Thankfully the infection cleared up and never returned. I continued to regularly brush his teeth to help overall.

Beemer's Tale 246

Have a Bite

When Beemer got the tooth infection we would cut up his food really small or give him soft foods so it was easier for him to eat. Just like a baby. He is my Baby Boy. After a few days Jack and I got a Bacon, Egg and Cheese sandwich for breakfast. I cut up a piece of mine, only the egg, cheese and bacon part, really small on a plate and gave it to him. Beemer did not want it. "What Beem you love bacon." Without thinking I took my sandwich and put it in front of him. "Do you want a bite?" Beemer took his own bite. We laughed. "Guess he is feeling better!" We let him continue to take bites of the sandwich. It was so fun to see him enjoy eating again.

Golden

A lot of people on our walks and even family or friends would say "You are spoiled Beemer." Our reply was always "NO, WE are spoiled for life with Beemer."

From day one when Beemer came to live with us he never had a bathroom accident in the house. He never chewed or ruined any furniture. He never stole food or shoes or sox. He never jumped on people. He never dug holes in the yard. He never ran away. He hardly ever barked even though we wished he would. Beemer is just a total joy to be around and everyone agreed.

Beemer never chased chipmunks, squirrels or birds to get them. Whenever the bunnies were in the yard Beemer would just stand and watch them. They were never afraid. On occasion when they started to run he would chase them but again never in an aggressive way;

it was only to play. The sweetest thing was when we found a baby bunny behind the garbage can. We found it when we moved the can to take out the garbage. Beemer came over to see what we were looking at. "Be gentle Beem. It's only a baby." He slowly walked closer and gave a gentle sniff. The baby was just laying there frozen not moving. The baby bunny never darted off as Beemer came over. So precious. I wished we had taken a picture of them together. "We have to leave him so his Mom will come get him." I said to Beemer. We put the garbage can back to protect him so no other bigger critters would get him. Later we checked and sure enough the Mom came back and the baby was gone.

Beemer's Friend - Baby Bunny

We had oak trees in both yards and Beemer never tried to eat the acorns. We had a crab apple tree at the new house and he never ate the apples; he only watched the squirrels as they ate them. Once in awhile he would pick up a stick not to eat but so we would chase him to get it if there wasn't a ball or toy handy.

Beemer is calm and sweet and helps others. Everyone loves him. Beemer is golden.

Work from Home

Initially when we moved in I set up my office down in the finished basement. We had one of those grey big industrial desks which Jack got from one of the jobs he worked on. When Beemer realized it wasn't Saturday he would come down and hang out with me on the couch across from the desk. It was a comfort to look over and see him there especially if work was stressful. "Time for Lunch Beem." We would go upstairs and eat. Then we would go for a walk after lunch on my lunch hour. In winter it was a little chilly down there so we had a space heater set up. In summer it was great as it was always cool down there.

After a few years we got a desk and set it up in our third bedroom which we called "Mikey's room." That is where Mikey slept whenever he came to stay with us. We ordered a dual desk so you could put two laptops on it. This way we could put our personal laptop one on one side and on the other side I could put my work laptop when working from home. When Mikey came to stay he had a place for his Ipad or game system and later his laptop.

So now on days when I would work from home I went into the Office/Mikey's Room instead of leaving. Beemer would come in and visit. "Hey Beem. There's my Best Boy in the World and Handsomest Guy in Town. Are you here to help me good boy? Thanks Beem." I would give him a hug. He would wag his tail maybe thinking it was Saturday but I didn't sing the Saturday song. Mikey's bed was in the office and we also put a cushioned bed for Beemer on the floor to hang out on for office visits. Beemer would lay on his bed or jump on Mikey's bed and hang out with me while I was working hoping for a walk break. "No worries Beem my Beauty I will take you on my lunch hour." Funny when people are on conference calls and you can hear babies crying or dogs barking. I never had to worry if on speaker phone since Beemer hardly every barked.

Getting Ready

Whenever it was time for walks I would go over to Beem on the couch and say "Beem you want to go to the park?" That would get his attention and he would pick his head up. "C'mon let's go." I would wave my hand. He immediately jumped off the couch and headed for the back slider doors.

On Saturday's or after work if I went to get changed Beem would hop off the couch before I got to go ask him. He would come to the walk-in closet and peek in. I said "You peekin my good boy? Yes I am getting changed. We are going." He would wait and as soon as I grabbed my sneakers he knew. He would wag his tail and turn around to head back to the kitchen to wait for me near the slider doors.

Often he would come to the bathroom door and if the door was open a crack he would look in to see if you were getting ready to take him for a walk. "You peekin again my good boy?" Beemer knew if I used the hairdryer that we were getting ready to go out without him. He would walk away and jump on the couch. If there was no hairdryer then he had hope he was going out.

We always felt so bad if we had to go out and leave him home. "Sorry Beem. We will be back in a little bit. You watch the house, that's your job my good boy. Thank You Beem. We love you." Both Jack and I always gave him a hug and a kiss before we left.

As we were walking out the door I would look back and say "Be back later Beem." He would always look so sad. Or sometimes he would start to get up and we had to say "No sorry Beem you can't come this time. We will go out later as soon as we get back." I felt guilty as he was so good everywhere we went but we could not take him when we were going out to dinner for a birthday or other occasion. I wished we could bring him like in England and the Pubs. The dogs were allowed if well behaved and would lay under the table. I could just picture Beemer coming with us and being so good. We often thought of sneaking him in as no one would ever know he was there since he hardly ever barked, but we didn't. We never wanted to jeopardize his Therapy Certification.

On our way home I would always say aloud "Hang in there Beem. We are on our way home." As we were approaching the house we could see he was sitting up looking out the window as if he knew. We would pull in the driveway and we could see him jump down off the couch to greet us at the door.

Jack's Birthday

Jack's birthday was in July so after we got Beemer his favorite way to celebrate was to go to the outside café with Beemer to have Burgers, Fries and Milkshakes. We would take Beemer to the Dog Beach first and then head over to the Burger Place on the corner of the Beach. I read that this was one of Bruce Springsteen's Dad's favorite spots. It was right across from the Inlet which leads out to the ocean. You can watch all the boats coming in and out. It is really a lovely spot. Hardest part was finding a parking spot if it was a nice day. If it was crowded we would park on a side street and walk to the Burger Place. All the times we went there we never saw Bruce, but we were happy to be there with Beemer. We would bring his towel and bowl for water. We would order and have "Lunch" outside. It was awesome. Happy Birthday Jack.

Number One - King Beemer

After we had Beemer for about 5 months everyone suggested "Why don't you get another dog so Beemer will have someone to play with and have company when you both are at work?" Jack and I were not sure at first. Yes Beemer was great with other dogs but did *we* want another one?

Beemer had his girlfriend Gizzy next door but since Gizzy was older she did not really run around as Beemer liked to do. They would just hang out together outside.

"What do you think?" I asked one night while we were sitting on the couch.

"I don't know. Beemer would probably love it but…I would do it for Beemer."

"Well let me just look online and see."

Fostering

I started looking online for dogs available for adoption. There was this one adorable brown terrier mix. Her name was Brooklyn. "Oh how cute that would be Brooklyn' and 'Beemer'. Can we go see her?" I asked Jack.

"Yeah I guess."

"Great. I will set it up."

We contacted Brooklyn's foster family. We filled out an application and sent via email and spoke on the phone. We agreed to meet them at the Pet Smart halfway between our house and theirs.

"Hi I am Louann and this is my husband Jack and this is Beemer."

"I am Debbie and this is Brooklyn."

We all shook hands. I immediately bent down to pet Brooklyn while Jack held Beemer. She was so sweet and gave me a kiss. Beemer came over to sniff Brooklyn. Brooklyn sniffed too.

"He is so friendly." Debbie said while petting Beemer. Debbie loved Beemer instantly.

Beemer and Brooklyn

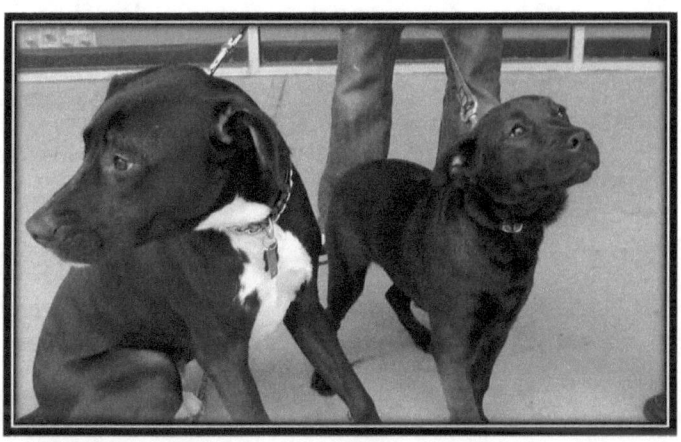

"Why don't we go over to the grass area and let them get better acquainted." Debbie suggested.

"Good idea." I replied.

We made our way over and Beemer of course wanted to play and got in his play stance. Brooklyn seemed interested and then kind of went after Beemer a little aggressively. We had to call him back.

"Brooklyn no." Debbie corrected.

"Well that's not a good start." Jack said.

"She is usually so good with all our dogs."

We let them walk around a little more but Brooklyn either snapped at Beemer if he came close or she stayed away.

"I don't think this is really a good match with Beemer. Such a shame. I am so sorry." I said. "Thank you so much for bringing Brooklyn."

"It was nice to meet you." Jack said.

"So sorry it didn't work out. She is really cute." I said.

"Yes me too. She is very sweet with people. I am sure she will find a good home." Debbie said.

"Yes I hope so." I said.

We gave Brooklyn a goodbye pet. "Bye Brooklyn."

"Bye Beemer. Take care." Debbie said.

"Thanks again." With that we headed home.

"Well guess it wasn't meant to be." Jack said in the car.

"Well it was only the first one."

"Just forget it."

"We'll see. I think it is worth another try." I said already planning to go back online when we got home.

I didn't have to wait long. Debbie sent an email.

"I am sorry that Brooklyn was a bit aggressive with Beemer, I was surprised because she does get along really well with my dogs. .... I have

attached a picture of Lucy. She is really submissive towards other dogs but she LOVES to play and play she will all day long. She has a very outgoing personality. We nicknamed her the lickey monster b/c she gives so many kisses. Let me know what you think.

Again, it was really nice meeting you."

Lucy

Lucy was cute as a button. Her name was originally 'Tiny Dancer.' They thought Lucy was a better fit. Lucy's coat was brown with black stripes just like my Mom's dog Pepper. Lucy is a Pit Bull/Boxer mix. "C'mon Jack, just take a look at her. Just take a look. Her coat is just like Pepper's. Please?"

Jack reluctantly came over. He leaned over my shoulder.

"Isn't she cute?"

"Yes she's cute."

"Let's just go see her." No answer. "Well how is this – if this doesn't work out then I'll drop it." That got his attention.

"Deal."

I emailed Debbie and she wrote back:

"Lucy is so easy to travel with I don't mind making the trip whenever you have the time. I am available during the days as well as the evenings except for Wed nights. If you fall in love with Lucy as I suspect you will, you have to promise to love her very much, she is something special. If I didn't have 2 dogs already I would keep her. I will only give her to a family that I know will love her this much. She is such a sweetheart! Talk to you soon!"

We made arrangements with Debbie to meet with Lucy at the same Pet Smart. We arrived first and we were standing out front with Beemer. We saw them pull up and Lucy got out of the car. "Oh there she is!" I said and pointed toward the car.

"Hi how are you doing?" I said.

"Good to see you again." Jack said.

"Yes good to see you too." I bent down to pet Lucy and she started licking my face.

"Oh she is a kisser. She loves to give kisses non-stop." Debbie said.

"I see." laughing as Lucy was still kissing my face.

Meeting Lucy

Beemer and Lucy seemed to really like each other. We walked over to the grassy area and after sniffing they wanted to run around together.

"I think they get along great don't you?" I said to Jack.

"Definitely they seem to get along."

I could tell Jack really liked her. We set a date for Debbie to come down to our house and leave Lucy for the weekend as a trial. We loved Lucy already but wanted to make sure it was the best thing for both Beemer and Lucy. In Debbie's email confirmation she wrote:

"And one other thing... Brooklyn has been adopted!"

We wrote back:

"Wonderful news about Brooklyn – that is really great!

See you next week!"

When they arrived we left Beemer inside as we wanted to give Lucy a chance to sniff around the yard.

"Hello Lucy." She trotted over with a tail wag.

"I'll go get Beemer." Jack said. Like a bullet Beemer came running right over to see Lucy. Both tails were wagging and Beemer immediately wanted to play. They ran around the oak tree and Beemer did his "Spin".

"I think we are off to a good start." I said smiling. "We'll send you email and pics on how they are doing over the weekend." Texting and cell phones were not the norm back then. Everything was thru emails.

"Great. You be good Lucy."

"Thanks again. Bye."

Beemer helped foster Lucy for the weekend. Beemer showed her to give paw, lie down and do a circle. It was so cute how she copied him.

We videotaped them playing and sleeping and doing tricks. We took tons of photos. Beemer was so fast that often we could not keep up with him with the video camera.

Beemer and Lucy Playing

Beemer's Tale 260

Beemer and Lucy Enjoying a Bone

By the end of the day they were both pooped and passed out on the couch.

I sent an email to Debbie.

"Just to let you know – all is well so far. They played until 1:30 and then came in for a snooze. Here are a few pictures. We actually got them to sit together for a treat. We'll try to get some sleep time pictures later. Have a nice weekend. Feel free to call anytime. Thanks so much again for giving us this opportunity!"

Debbie replied.

"Thanks so much for the wonderful pictures as well as the update! Please do send more, I love to see them! By the way my Husband said Beemer is beautiful!!!

Have a Great Weekend and I will talk to you soon!"

Beemer and Lucy Sitting Together

The next day they were busy playing again. Lucy came over and Jack started to pet her. Beemer came over and cut in line for a pet. "I think he might be a little jealous."

"Really?" I said.

At bedtime this confirmed Jack's observation. Both Lucy and Beemer jumped on the bed. Beemer made sure he had pole position between Jack and I and Lucy was at the end of the bed. In the morning everyone had all tail wags and Lucy came over kissing my face. "Good morning everybody." I said. Beemer sat right next to Jack's head. "Beemer what are you doing my boy?" Jack said. Beemer definitely had to be the closest.

We loved our weekend of fostering. We thanked Debbie so much again for letting us have the chance with Lucy. We thought it over and really were not sure it was right for Beemer. We really did love Lucy but knew because she was so sweet she would get a good home. Beemer had to be Number One. And we were good with that.

We kept in contact with Debbie via email checking in on Lucy and giving updates on Beemer. One time we even got to watch Lucy when Debbie and Joe went away which was great.

I sent an email to Debbie:

"Beemer is starting class for Pet Therapy..... How is Miss Lucy? We think of her often."

Debbie's reply:

"I am glad to hear you are all doing well. Beemer will make a wonderful dog for pet therapy someday!

She has a sweet gentle soul.... But tons and tons of energy... but you already know that! But we love her anyway.

Keep in touch... let me know how Beemer does in therapy school!"

Next update.

"Lucy is doing well, wowing people with all of her new tricks thanks to you guys!... Joe and I decided that we are going to adopt her....She thinks our home is her home, we have had her for almost 4 months which is the longest I have ever had any foster and we love her."

We replied.

"Congratulations on getting Lucy! We know she will be really happy with you guys and it makes us feel better too.....

Wanted to let you know that Beemer completed his course and he is now a Certified Pet Therapy Dog! We are really proud of him."

We were so happy that Debbie and Joe were adopting Lucy. She really is so sweet and we could tell how much they love her. We know Lucy has a terrific home.

Our last email from Debbie was a year later.

"I just wanted to say Hello. I hope this email finds you well. I have attached some pics of Lucy. She turned 2 and graduated from dog obedience this past September! Give Beemer kisses for us!

Write back."

It was such a nice surprise to hear from them. We often think of Debbie, Joe and Lucy. We love Lucy and so enjoyed our time together. The pictures were adorable of Lucy with her Birthday cake. Lucy's picture was even on the cake. Awesome.

"So great to hear from you! Thank you so much for sending us the pictures of Lucy. She is absolutely adorable! That is really terrific she graduated. The cake is great – bet she loved it. We think of her often. We are going to print the pictures and show them to the kids across the street. They often ask about Lucy.

Hope all is well with you too. Beemer is doing good – we are still taking him to Agility which he loves. Attached is a picture of Beemer on the *beach and also holding his favorite ball. Give Lucy a big hug and kiss from us! Hope you have and wonderful Holiday!"*

I had read that if you get another dog then it can change their personality a bit as now they have to share attention. We never wanted to change Beemer's personality in any way. Beemer deserved to be number one.

Instead we minded other friends and family member's dogs so he got to play but it was temporary so when they went home he regained the throne.

Whenever Jack's Mom did not feel well we would bring Pepi over so she did not have to keep getting up to let him out or worry about feeding him. Pepi and Beemer would run in the yard together. Sometimes Beemer would get a little 'Jelly" as Jack called it if we gave Pepi too much attention. Beemer would come over and put his head in your lap as if to say "Don't forget about me." "How could we ever forget about you Beemer? You are Number One. Pepi is just visiting." We would tell him.

Beemer never showed any sign of conflict. With toys and bones he would let other dogs take his toys or bones without a question. It was amazing to see how he would let them and would just sit and watch. Sometimes he would let out a little whine but never tried to take it back. Once they were done then he would go and pick it up.

On one of our Vet visits, one of techs was walking outside with a cute dog with a brindle coat about

Beemer's size. "Aww he is so cute what is his name?" I said.

"His name is Nacho and he is up for adoption." she replied.

"Aww he seems so nice."

"He could make a good friend for Beemer."

"Sorry Beemer has to be King."

She smiled and said "Yes Beemer is King."

King Beemer

Running with the Marines

My Father was in the Merchant Marines. Jack's Father was an Army Veteran. Our nephew, who is Jack's brother's son, joined the marines when he graduated high school. Every time he came to visit he would take Beemer for a run. "Hey Beemer is running with the Marines." Jack would say.

"Yes he is." I said. I turned to Beemer. "Beemer you are still in training kid, but this time you are training with the Marines."

Our nephew went on to be promoted, served in Afghanistan and even worked on the Presidential HMX1 Helicopters. We are very proud of him.

We have total respect for all who serve. We thank them all.

Farmer's Market

Every Sunday during the summer we went to the Farmer's Market in town. Of course Beemer was along for the ride. Everyone stopped to pet him or ask about him. We became friends with one of the workers at the vegetable stand.

"There's Beemer." Cathy would say and immediately come over to see him. She would tell us about her dog. "Nellie is getting older too and likes to sleep a lot."

"Yes we keep trying to keep him going and take him out."

"Any time you want to bring him to the farm you can come and let him run around."

"Aww that is so nice. Thank you."

One man called him over and Beemer came with a tail wag. The man bent down to pet him and said "Hi there fella – you wear your gray as a mask of honor." Oh wow I thought. "Yes he does. He is a Therapy Dog." I said.

Then several little girls walked over and said "Can we pet your dog?"

"Sure. Just be gentle as he is getting over a tooth infection. He is very friendly."

They were so respectful as they lightly touched his back. "What's his name?" "How old is he?" My usual response. "This is Beemer. He is 14 and he is my teenager." And they giggled.

We also made friends with the lady at the booth who sold Dog and Cat Treats. She made them herself and always offered Beemer a treat. "He has allergies so it is hard for us to give him treats as most have chicken in them."

"I have just the thing for him. Here try these. They are dried sweet potato." And she handed us a couple.

"What do we owe you?"

"No that's okay. See if he likes them and then if so you can buy some next time."

That was really so sweet. "Thank you so much. We will definitely let you know."

When we got home we gave Beemer one. He liked it and layed happily on the couch chewing his sweet potato treat. "Hey this is great." I said to Jack. "He likes it."

Well that lasted a day. The next day he wanted nothing to do with the sweet potato treat to our dismay. Beemer often only liked things when they were new.

My sister came for a visit and we gave one of the sweet potato treats to her little dachshund mix Pepper. "She loves everything." My sister laughed. So next trip to the Farmer's Market we bought sweet potato treats for Pepper.

<u>Elvis Impression</u>

Beemer developed a little twitch or shake in one of his back legs. We brought him to the Vet and they said it was nothing to be concerned about that it was just a muscle twitch. When we were out and people would notice they would say "Aww he must be cold." If it was nice out "Oh he must be scared."

We assured them otherwise. "No he is fine. That is just his Elvis Impression." We always got a laugh with that one.

Chapter 17 – Parks, Parades and Parties – Part 2

<u>Beemer's Favorite Days</u>

I often wonder what Beemer thought his favorite days are. I think it was when we took him to a big open field or the dog beach where he could run freely without any boundaries or restrictions. He could run until he got tired out.

Yes he loved when we got to go on two walks a day or when we were out all day or evening at an event, but being able to run free you could see the look on his face. Maybe because he was so confined so long in the shelter, six months for a puppy is a long time. We definitely tried to make up for it.

Dog Beach

Beemer loves the dog beach. There is a very long area of beach where he could run. Beemer would run from one end and back and got to play with other dogs in between. We felt he was so happy being there. After he got tired out we brought him home gave him a bath and then it was time for a snooze.

Going in the Water

This one time when the dogs were chasing him someone threw a ball in the water. All the dogs started to run after it. Beemer looked back and saw them running toward the water. He turned and followed them. They were all running so fast and he was trying to catch up to be in the lead and all of a sudden he found himself in the water. He stopped dead in his tracks. Looked left and right and then spun around running out of the water toward us. "OMG he actually went in the water! Get the towel Jack."

"Hey Beem. Good boy you were in the water! That's great." I said.

"Good boy Beem." Jack said.

Beemer did a big shake and we dried him off laughing. That was the one and only time Beemer went in the water at the Dog Beach.

Message in the Bottle

We loved to watch Beemer run and play with the other dogs at the Dog Beach. This one day in mid October 2006 it was unseasonably warm. "It is too nice today – let's take Beemer to the dog beach." Jack agreed and off we went. At the time we got there it happened to be low tide and it was a very low tide. You could walk out halfway to the middle of where the water was usually. Since Beemer was never a fan of the water; he would stop right at the water's edge and never go in. We coaxed Beemer to go out as far as possible till the water started. There were all kinds of treasures to be found there since it was usually covered by water. We found lovely pieces of sea glass.

Beemer at the Water's Edge

"Hey look at this." Jack yelled. I walked over to where Jack was standing. It was a dog tag with a name and address. 'Winston.' "Oh wow – he must have lost it while running in the water." Jack kept it and put it in his pocket.

When we got home Jack said "I am going to send it back to them. I don't think we will get anything back but I know if it was Beemer's I would be happy someone sent it back."

"That is a great idea. So cool. Like our very own version of Sting's 'Message in a Bottle'. Let's do it."

Jack packaged up the tag with a note signed from Beemer.

We never really expected to get any response. To us it was just fun. Three days before Beemer's birthday we received the following note in the mail addressed to Beemer.

> *Hi –*
>
> *We are very grateful for the tag being returned. Thank you for caring. Winston is "Delighted" to know if he gets lost the tag will help him get back home.*
>
> *Best Wishes,*
>   *"Winston"*

We were surprised someone took the time to send a Thank You. Another interesting thing was that Winston and his family lived an hour north of the Dog Beach in the same town that my Grandparents lived before they moved here and where my sister currently works today. We kept the letter. We put it in Beemer's file of keepsakes.

Across the bay from the dog beach there were two waterfront restaurants with outdoor seating. Depending on what time we went sometimes they would have live music. Often we would hang out to listen as you could hear great across the water while Beemer got to run and play with the other dogs.

John's cousin Joey and his wife Kelly live in Florida. It was so thoughtful whenever there was a storm predicted to be coming on the news they would call us. On several occasions they actually called us while we were with Beemer at the Dog Beach. We would answer and tell them about the conditions here while we were walking with Beemer.

Fog

I remember one time we went to the Dog Beach. It was a warm and clear day at our house. "It's a perfect day for the Dog Beach today." I said to Jack. When we got there it was like we were in a different place. It was so foggy you could hardly see a foot in front of you. Since we were there we decided to go down to the beach. It was eerie. Hardly anyone was there so it was kind of nice we had the beach to ourselves. We could let Beemer off the leash. Beemer loved it. Only problem was when he ran ahead we could not see him. "Beem wait!" I would call. Beemer would wait for us until we could catch up.

Beemer's Tale 278

Polar Bear Plunge - 2007

It was January but it was sunny and the day was not that cold so I took Beemer down to the Dock. I put on his coat and off we went. We drove down just to break him out of the house for a different place to sniff. When we got to the Dock no one was there so I let Beemer off the leash. He went to smell around and there was a big group of ducks along the shore where the kayaks and canoes launch off. Since Beemer liked to walk there along the reeds he went down. Since he is so calm and never tries to chase them they usually just go in the water and move away from him. For some reason they got spooked today and made a flutter and a mad dash to go in the water. Beemer was startled and jumped in after them. "Beem No!" I could not believe he went in. "Beem. Beem. Come here." He jumped out of the water.

I was frantic as I did not want him to get too cold as the water was ice cold. I took off his coat which was soaked and started to wipe him down with my scarf. I made a mad dash to the car, started it and turned the heat up on high. I opened the passenger door and pointed. "Beem come." He came right over and jumped in the backseat. Luckily we always kept a towel in the trunk just in case and I ran to get it and started drying him off and wrapped it around him. "Beem we got to go home." We went home as fast as we could. I was so worried he would get hyperthermia. "Thank God we drove today Beem." I said to him.

When we got home we burst in and I said to Jack "Get towels and blankets – Beemer jumped in the water!"

"What? Beemer never goes in the water."

"I know! I know, but he did!"

We got towels and dried him off even more and covered him with a blanket. Shortly after a rest we gave him a nice warm bath. We just could not believe it. Beemer officially joined the Polar Bear Club. Too bad he did not have a sponsor.

Fireworks

We have a lot of events with Fireworks near our house that you can hear from a distance. At the beach every Thursday in the Summer they have Fireworks. Before the Fireworks show they would have a band come and play at the Bandshell which was in a small field in front of the beach. Jack's one friend actually booked all the bands to play and we would go a little early so Jack could help his friend set up. We went very often to the Bandshell Concerts and Fireworks with Beemer and met other friends there as well. We met so many people we knew there and made new friends. We became friends with one of the owner's of the motel across the street from the park. Every week the owner and his wife would say 'Hi' and come over to see us and Beemer.

We brought Beemer a blanket, a bone and bowl of water and he hung out with us. Beemer never seemed phased by the Fireworks. We would walk around a few times around the field during the night if he seemed like he was bored but when the Fireworks went off he was fine which was great.

One time our friend Jeannie and her Mom came. Jack knew Jeannie from his home town when we met.

Jeannie moved down here but her Mom, Lily, still lived up north. For awhile Jack and Jeannie would commute to work together up north and then Jeannie retired. Once retired Jeannie traveled a lot. In earlier days Jeannie was a cruise director like on the 'Love Boat'. So she returned to cruising but now for vacation. She was known as the 'Cruise Queen'. Since she traveled so much she did not have a pet and her Mom Lily was not well enough to take care of a pet of her own so Beemer would fill in for hugs and fun.

The night they came to the fireworks it was oldies night. Jeanne's Mom, Lily, loved to dance and was tapping her foot to one of the songs. Jack walked over and said "Will you dance with me Lily my Lily." She was so happy and they danced. Beemer got up and wagged his tail. So I decided to dance with Beemer. We danced by doing circles and then he sat down and did his sit up trick. "Aww thank you Beem. Yes I would love this dance." I took his paws gently in my hands and we swayed a bit and did our own dance for a minute.

All those times we went Beemer was never afraid of the fireworks. The noise never bothered him. Then one day we were walking back to our house at the end of the street. A short distance away some kids were lighting firecrackers. We heard a 'Boom' and Beemer bolted. It must have been an M80. It was very loud. Beemer took off running and I could not keep up. "Beem it's okay." He pulled on the leash and his collar popped off and went flying. I grabbed his collar off the ground and ran after him. He went directly to our house. We tried to comfort him and make sure he was okay. He took a drink of water and we gave him some treats. After that day Beemer never liked fireworks anymore just like Thunder.

Later when we tried to put his collar back on we noticed that his ID tag was missing. It was very distinctive. It was a blue dog bone shape with his name address and phone number. We walked back down the end of the street but it was already dark and we could not find it.

The next day Jack told the kids next door what happened and asked them to help us look for it. "I'll give you 5 bucks if you find it."

"Five bucks?" they said in unison.

"Well forget it that's not enough. Just get him a new one."

Our reaction was 'Wow'. When we were kids we would have been running down the street to look. Yes we could definitely get him a new one but we liked that one. Funny how times have changed. Jack and I did go back down the street ourselves and luckily we found it.

Dragged through the Mud

It had rained for several days in a row so we hadn't gone to the park. When the sun finally showed we took advantage and went to the Community Park. They had several softball fields, but Beemer and I always walked along the path around them. Beemer had extra energy to burn off since being cooped up inside because of the rain. He decided to take off across the soccer field which was between the two softball fields. "Beem it's too wet." Of course I went running with him. The grass was all soggy and squishy. "Eww Really Beem?" You could see the water flying each time we set our foot down. He was having fun so I let him run. Beemer suddenly made a sharp right and was heading directly for the softball field. "Beem what are you doing?" I slipped cause my sneakers were so wet and I dropped the leash. Beemer continued dead on straight ahead right across the softball field. "Beemer no – Wait!" He stopped dead in his tracks as he always did on the command "Wait" but it was too late his paws were covered in mud and the leash was a mess after being dragged through the mud. "Oh My God Beem." I started laughing. I couldn't be mad. He looked like a little kid wanting to play in the mud. Even I remember making mud pies with my sister. "Jack is going to kill us." Then I walked over. "Good boy Beem." That was for waiting and not for going through the mud. I took Beemer the shortest distance to get off the softball field. I had a towel in the car to wipe off most of the mud from Beemer's feet and I put the leash in a plastic bag. "Well hope you enjoyed yourself. You know what this means Beem? It's going to be bath time when we get home." I don't think he liked the sound of that as he knew what the word 'bath' meant.

<u>Praise</u>

Beemer got kudos and praise wherever he went. One person on the next block whenever we would walk by would run over and say "Beemer. So good to see you." She would drop to her knees and hug and kiss him.

We know Beemer is great but all the attention he receives and gets wherever we goes is truly fabulous and well deserved. He is so receptive and happy to see everyone. We are so proud of him.

So many people tell him how 'cute', 'adorable', and how 'handsome' he is. I know lots of family and friends who have dogs and they do not nearly get the amount of comments that Beemer receives almost daily. He is very unique and one of a kind.

Compliments

The following are some of the compliments and comments he received most often:

Number One question – "What kind of dog is he?"

"He's a good looking dog."

"He is a really beautiful dog."

"He is handsome."

"He is so cute."

"He is so sweet."

"I love the white feet." Our reply "He always has his sneakers on."

"He is really well behaved."

"He is so well trained."

"Hi cute doggie."

"He has such a cute face."

"He is in such good shape."

"You must really take good care of him."

Whenever Beemer got a compliment we always thanked them and explained how he is a Rescue and a Therapy Dog.

This one time we were walking in the park, soccer practice just finished and all the kids were walking off the field toward the parking lot with their parents. A lot of the kids would stop and comment "Hi doggie." "What a cute dog." And often some would stop to pet him. There was this one little girl, cute as a button with dark curly hair. She was probably about 5 or 6 years old. "Can I pet your dog?" she asked.

"Sure. He is very friendly."

"What's his name?"

"This is Beemer. He is a Therapy Dog. He visits patients in the hospital. He was rescued from the shelter." There were several smiles from the kids standing by.

" Do you have any pets?" I asked

"Yes we have a cat named Murphy."

"Nice. Well Beemer likes cats too."

"I like dogs."

Her Mom then called her over. "Thanks for letting me pet your dog."

"You are welcome. Have a good day."

She waved bye and started to run toward her Mom. Then she turned around and ran back toward us. She stopped and put her hand on her hip. "I just have to say. Your dog is very well behaved."

I laughed out loud. "Why thank you. Yes he has had a lot of training."

She waved bye again and ran off. I thought that was really something this little girl had so much conviction in her statement and that she just had to let us know. "Beemer even as a teenager you still got it kid!"

Another time we were walking on the track in front of the parking lot at the Beach Park. A young girl and a young man got out of their car. They opened the back door and out jumped an adorable Labradoodle. "Oh look Beem isn't he cute?" I said out loud to Beemer. The girl turned toward us and said "My boyfriend or my dog?" I laughed "Both." She smiled "Yes they are and so is yours."

Children

Children flocked to Beemer. Even the children on our block who had pets of their own would come over to see Beemer. Kerri and Colin had a son, Evan, a few years after their daughter Lizzy was born. They also got a second Pug named Rocky to be a playmate for Mugsy. When Lizzy and Evan got older they would fly out their front door to see Beemer as we walked by. I thought that was so funny how they had two dogs of their own but they wanted to see Beemer. "Can we walk him?" they would ask.

"Sure you can take him around your lawn."

I would hand them the leash and Beemer would walk with them sniffing the trees on their lawn. After a bit I would say "Ok we are going to go to the park now."

"Ohhhh not yet." They would say.

"Okay a few more minutes." It was so sweet.

Whenever we had friends over with their children, all the kids loved to run and chase Beemer. Just like at the

BBQs it was so fun to watch and you would hear their high pitched cries of laughter whenever Beemer did "The Spin." Sometimes the kids would crash into each other trying to turn to go in Beemer's new direction.

Chasing Beemer

One time Jack was walking up the corner and he turned down the alley way behind the Chinese restaurant. A young boy was walking toward them and stopped "That is a really beautiful dog." "Thank you." Jack said. "His name is Beemer – he is a Therapy Dog. " The boy petted Beemer and said "Awesome." "Have a good day." Jack said. "You too. Have a good day Beemer."

Parties

All the people's houses we went and parties over the years they always said without us even asking "Beemer is welcome." Our friend Lenny often emailed or texted us to come to a party or if he was playing music and to bring Beemer if it was an outside event. Lenny said "Come for the day. Beemer is welcome."

One time Lenny sent us a text.

> *"Pig roast tomorrow. Bring Beemer and come up. Perfect weather! Love L."*

Lenny said we could all stay over at his place.

Everyone is amazed how calm and adapting Beemer is. Beemer is just happy to be going. After we told people he was rescued from the shelter many people would say "Beemer you are lucky you have a good home." We replied "No. We are the lucky ones."

Bird Sanctuary

Beemer is 13. We went on a winter's day for a walk. It was sunny and 45 degrees in February. We went to the Sanctuary. It was great. We walked. We ran and then got to the Sanctuary. Along the path there was a huge log blocking the path. I yelled "Jump" like we did in Agility but it was too soon. Beemer jumped but took a tumble. My heart sank to see him fall to the ground face first because of my command. I felt so bad I yelled too soon. I started to run over to see if he was ok. He quickly got up and shook and darted to the left of the path. I finally caught up to Beemer. He kept licking his chops and nose. I saw his nose was covered in mud. "Oh Beem I am so sorry." He was trying to breathe to get the mud off. I had tissues in my fanny pack which I took on our walks. I wiped off his nose. He shook his head to the left and then to the right. Just like a little kid when you are trying to wipe off their face with a napkin.

He then ran off. "Hey! Beem wait!" I watched as he stopped as that was our command to stop and wait. He seemed ok. "Thank You!" Beemer never liked his nose or face wiped. Beemer and I had so many wonderful walks we shared in the Sanctuary; we love going to the Sanctuary together. This was just one glitch. Moments whether seconds or minutes; those are what are captured in your heart and you remember.

Parties at Sam's

Even when we moved across the street Beemer always knew when our neighbor Sam would have a party. Just like he did when we lived next door Beemer would look out the window and see all the cars pull up and the people go over to Sam's house. Every time we went to the door Beemer jumped off the couch. We had a second refrigerator in the garage so often we would have to go out to get something for what we were bringing over to Sam's for the party. I would raise my hand and say "Not yet Beem. Don't worry you are going to the party." Then he would just jump back on the couch and patiently wait. When we were finally ready "Okay Beem. Party time." He would fly off the couch and go right to the door. We let him out and opened the garage door. Beemer would wait at the end of the driveway. We always taught him 'no street without a leash'. We would hook up his leash and with tail wagging Beemer would head over automatically to Sam's house.

Beemer Playing with Toys in Sam's Yard

Park Therapy Visits

Henry

God bless Henry. He was in his 70s and every day it was nice we would see him walking. He lived on the next street. He carried weights and would do his boxing moves with the weights like Sylvester Stallone in "Rocky". We became good friends over the years. He always stopped to talk to us when we saw him on his block or ours. It was like a Pet Therapy visit as Henry was always so happy to see Beemer. "How you doing Beemer?" and he would bend down to pet him. "It's good to get exercise."

"You are so right. Every day we try to go just like you." I would reply with a smile.

I remember the first time we met. I saw a man probably in his early 70's raking leaves on his front lawn. As Beemer and I passed by he stopped raking and leaning on his rake he said "I see you guys pass by all the time. That's a good looking dog you got there. What's his name?"

"Hi. His name is Beemer. Say Hi Beemer." I led Beemer over to him. He bent down and pet Beemer. "What a good boy. We have cats. My wife is afraid of dogs."

"Oh well cats are great too. Beemer is really friendly. He is even friends with our neighbor's cat."

"Really? Well he seems like a great one."

"He is and we do Pet Therapy where he visits patients in Assisted Living Facilities."

"That's terrific. He is like a service dog then."

"Yes he is. I am Louann by the way. We live on the next block."

"I am Henry."

"Nice to meet you Henry. I see you have your work cut out for you there. We better let you get back to the leaves. I am sure we will see you again."

"Yes yes. Will look for you as you walk by."

"Great. Bye. Say good bye Beemer." And with a wag we continued to the park.

Ever since that day we have been friends with Henry. We would see him often on our trip around the block or on our way to the park.

One day Henry was walking down our street. "Hi Henry how are you doing today?" Jack asked.

"Hi doing good. Doing good. Today is my 80th birthday."

"Oh wow Happy Birthday." Jack said.

"That is terrific! Happy Birthday!" I said.

"Thank you. Feeling pretty good. And how's our boy doing today?" Beemer went right over and Henry bent down to pet Beemer.

"Such a good dog and handsome too. Really in great shape."

"Just like you." I said. Henry laughed. "Not like him but I am doing."

"Looking good. Stay that way." Jack said.

"I'm trying."

"You are. Hope you have a great birthday. What are you doing to celebrate?" I added.

"We are going out to dinner with our daughter."

"Excellent." I said.

"Enjoy – you deserve it. But remember you are what you eat." Jack said.

Henry smiled. "I'll try to remember that."

After chatting about other events and the weather we said our goodbyes.

"So good to see you." I said.

"You too, you too."

"Have a great day and birthday." Jack said.

"Thanks and you do the same. Bye Beemer." Henry waved and went on his way.

Beatle Bob

On the next block over when we would do a short walk we passed Beatle Bob's house. He was an older gentleman who lived alone. We called him Beatle Bob as he had a haircut that looked like the early Beatles and his name really was Bob. On the occasions where he was outside and saw us he would come over. He was usually raking his lawn. "Hi how are you doing?"

"Nice today."

"Yes it is. Whenever it is nice Beemer is always ready for a walk."

"He is a good dog." he would reply looking at Beemer and then stroke his back.

"Well don't work too hard. Have a good day."

"You too. Bye."

Beatle Bob was not a man of many words but we were happy to see him and wish him well.

Mikey

When my nephew, my sister's son, Mikey was older he would come to stay with Jack and I by himself for a few days during the summer. We all went on walks together. We would have our usual people we know stop to say hi or new people asking about Beemer while on our walks. When we got home Mikey said "Wow you know everybody."

I laughed "Yes Beemer knows a lot of people. We walk almost every day."

My sister always took their dogs for walks in the morning before school started and Mikey was still asleep and did not go. Also since it was so early my sister said there was hardly anyone outside at that time. It was a treat for Mikey to come with us and also Mikey got to enjoy the park.

To think we would never have met so many wonderful people and/or their pets and became friends over the years if it was not for Beemer.

Experiment

Studies suggest that when you smile it makes you feel better. You release endorphins when you smile and it makes those around you feel better too. When we went to the park on Saturday mornings we would see this older gentleman walking slowly around the track. When we got close by I would always say "Hi how are you?" with a smile. We were met with no response. "Hmmm okay." I said to Beemer. "We are going to make it our mission to make him smile Beem." Weeks went by. Every time we would see him I would smile and say the same "Hi" or "Good Morning how are you?" No response.

One day we were on our usual walk and we saw him. "Okay Beem we are going to try again." As we approached I said my usual with a smile. I got back half a smile and he kept going. "That's a start. Yes Beem we did it!" Then Beemer and I took off on a run of victory.

Chapter 18 – Friends and Family – Part 2

Beemer definitely has a human-like quality. Jack and I would say how Beemer yawns like Jack's Dad. He tilts his head back and lets out a loud yawn noise. Beemer gives us those sad eyes whenever he cannot come with us and puts his head down between his front paws like a pout. When it is time to go somewhere Beemer's eyes light up and he dances around the door like a little kid. When we are in the car he lets out little whines sometimes as if to say "Are we there yet?" How we wish those words he gives us with his eyes could be spoken. Human-like or not Beemer is a real member of the family.

One of the aids on our visits said "He is so calm just like a person." When our friends would come over Alan would always say when we were all sitting in the living room "He hangs out just like he is one of us." Beemer would often pick his head up from laying on the couch and turn his head and look at whoever was talking like he was interested in the conversation. My sister-in-law said "I tell everyone about him. He is such a good boy and handsome. He seems so human." Our friend Lenny even said "Beemer must have been a human in a former life."

<u>Coffee Shop</u>

>Beemer is welcomed everywhere. Because he is a Certified Therapy Dog he was even welcomed at the Coffee Shop. We knew the owner and she knew Beemer. The owner, Sarah, dated our friend Lenny and we went to several dinners at her home. She would say "Bring Beemer – please." Beemer was so gentle with Sarah's dog Maggie who was an older black Lab.

One day when we were walking by the coffee shop after going to the Farmer's Market Jack said "I want to go in and get some coffee to bring home."

"Okay. I can wait here with Beemer."

When Sarah saw us she immediately came to the door. "Come in. Come in."

"I wasn't sure if we should bring Beemer in."

"Of course he is welcome." In we went and we got a small table in the corner. Beemer layed down under the table. No one even knew he was there until someone spotted him and then people wanted to pet him. He would wag his tail and they would bend down and pet him. We got a muffin and gave Beemer a bite. It was Beemer's first visit to the coffee shop and he didn't even drink coffee.

Mail Carriers

The stigma of dogs and Mail Carriers. Not sure if it is the uniform or someone unknown coming to the house every day that drives some dogs crazy. Beemer is an exception.

When we lived at my Grandparent's house we had Ellen as our Mail Carrier. She was a very pretty young lady and all the men in the neighborhood took notice. Jack knew her Dad who made deliveries to his Uncle's Gas Station and so we had a connection. Ellen met Beemer after he first came to live with us. "He is so handsome." He came right up to greet her.

"Say hi Beemer." He did with a wag. Again Beemer made an instant friend. He never barked when she came by he would just look out the window and wag his tail . Beemer was just happy to see Ellen; someone he knew. Every day that Beemer was outside Ellen would stop to see him. She would kneel down and give him a hug. Jack said "Man thought she was happy to see me, but she was happy to see Beemer."

After we moved across the street Ellen got reassigned. We really missed her as she was so great and we considered her a friend. We got a new Mail Carrier. Turns out it was the Brother-In-Law of one of Sam's ex-girlfriends. Here was another connection. We introduced Beemer to Jimmy. Beemer also welcomed him as a new friend. We became very close with Jimmy. We always offered him something to drink; his favorite was 'YooHoo'. He would stop for a minute to get a drink and visit with us and Beemer. We would ask about his wife whom we knew and their two sons. The boys are so adorable and we have seen them many times. We shared pet stories as they also had dogs.

When we saw Jimmy making deliveries in his Mail Truck on our walks he always yelled in a deep voice 'Beeeeemer'. Beemer looked over and recognized it was Jimmy and wagged his tail. So sweet and I waved. I called out "Jack's home – go get a refreshment."

Jack got to know Doug, the UPS driver, from delivering over the last 20 years. "Hey Doug how are you doing?"

"Good. Got a package for you."

"Thanks."

"How's the pooch?"

"Doing good – I'll let him say hello." Jack opened the door and let Beemer out.

"He is so friendly."

"He loves everybody." Jack said. Doug was another welcome visitor in Beemer's eyes.

Beemer never barked or was flustered from people in uniform, deliveries, or Mail Carriers. They were all friends and welcomed. He never took a bite, he only showed the love.

Crabbing

Whenever our musician friend Lenny came down to visit he loved to go crabbing and his ritual of going to the beach before Sundown. He even wrote a song about it. "Take me to the Water before the Sun goes Down." He describes hanging out in our garage for dinner with Beemer, Jack and I.

On a few occasions Jack and I would go crabbing with Lenny and bring Beemer with us. Beemer had no problem walking on the dock or boardwalk so we thought it would be fun to hang out for awhile. As we were walking down the dock as soon as the dock lead over the water Beemer started to slow down. "What's the matter Beem?" I looked down and his feet were spread flat out like a duck's foot. You could see his webbed toes. "OMG Jack look!" I pointed to Beemer's feet.

Jack started laughing. "Wow. Guess he doesn't like being over the water." It was hilarious at poor Beemer's expense.

"It's okay Beem. We are not going in." I said. We made our way slowly down the rest of the dock till we got to the end.

"You gotta get a picture of that." Jack said. I took out my phone and took a picture. We then put a blanket down so Beemer could lay down. Once he could not see the water between the slats he relaxed.

Beemer's Webbed Lab Foot

"Good boy. You are crabbing." Lenny said. We hung out for awhile. It was so relaxing and pretty to watch the boats go by. When I thought Beemer had enough I said "I am going to take Beemer home for his dinner. I will meet you guys back at the house."

"Sure okay. Probably a good idea." Jack said.

"Good Luck." I said.

"See you later Beem." Lenny said.

Every time we took Beemer crabbing it was the same. It was the only time his webbed feet made an appearance. Beemer really is a Lab who doesn't like the water.

Beemer's Tale 302

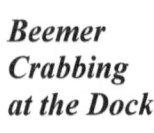
Beemer Crabbing at the Dock

Catch of the Day

This one day we walked down to the Dock. Beemer would always hop down where the canoes and kayaks launch and walk along the water's edge next to the reeds. A very large fish had washed ashore and he went right up to it to sniff. I could not resist so I took a picture of him sniffing the fish. When we got home I showed it to Jack. "Look what Beemer caught."

Jack looked at the picture. "What? He didn't catch that."

I was going to play along and try and convince him otherwise but he knew Beemer too well. "No but I thought it was funny. I am going to send it to Lenny as a joke."

"That's great! You should send it to Ken too."

"Oh yeah. Ken's the big deep sea fisherman. He will love it." I texted the picture to Lenny and Ken and a few other friends with the caption "Catch of the Day."

Instant responses back. "Did he really catch it? "

My response "Beemer caught his own dinner." I couldn't resist.

"Awesome." Ken texted back.

"Go Beemer." Lenny texted back.

Beemer's Tale 304

Car Shows

A good friend of mine from work, Joe, is very big into restoring and working on vintage cars. Every year they have a big car show near our house. Jack, Beemer and I always go to see him and walk around to see the cars. Joe's favorite car he restored is his Pink Cadillac. It is really beautiful. He has even had offers for people to take pictures in it for their wedding. Joe gives us a tour of all the highlights and facts about the cars. It really is fun. People would stop to pet Beemer and ask his name. Since Beemer's name represents a prized possession like a vintage car; our response is "We may not have a car like yours but at least we have a 'Beemer'." That always was a hit. There are vendors at the event that sell hot dogs and hamburgers so we always got Beemer one. We take pictures with Beemer near all the fun cars we know he would love to ride in.

Beemer at the Car Show

Snippet

Dean was my hairdresser for years. Turns out we were connected from up North and Jack's hometown when we met. We went to many of the same restaurants and clubs. We probably ran into him and didn't know him yet. Gerry and I had the same hairdresser. Too funny. Gerry loved Dean. So do we. Dean always had jokes and funny stories to share. He made you look forward to getting your haircut and talking with him. He was thee Grand Poobah at one of the Local Lodges for several years and also was very involved in several of the Churches in town and ran numerous events to raise money and help people.

One time Gerry patted his tummy and said "Hey you are gaining a little weight."

Dean's reply "My Father always said if you are proud of something build a roof over it." Gerry loved that one.

This one time we went to Riverfront Park we were walking toward the Picnic Area. We heard a familiar voice loud and clear. "Beemer!" As we got closer we heard the voice say "I know this dog. He is awesome." It was Dean. Dean was having a BBQ with friends. They had Sausage and Peppers on the grill and were playing Bocci. Beemer's nose was definitely interested.

"Hey how are you?" I said as we got closer.

"How are you doing man? Jack asked.

"Great. Do you guys want to join us?" Dean said.

"Oh thanks so much, but maybe next time." I said.

"Well we are here every Monday. We play Bocci and cook out if the weather is good."

"That is awesome." I said.

"Yes we will definitely try to come." Jack said.

"Have fun and Enjoy." And we said our Goodbyes.

Bennyfest

Our musician friend Lenny came down every summer for 10 days vacation. We call it Bennyfest since he lives an hour and a half up north. "Lenny the Benny" we call him as Bennies were anyone who lived up North and came to the Jersey Shore for the summer. We would have a great time when he came down. He always stayed with Sam until we moved across the street and had more room. Then Lenny would alternate between staying with Sam or us. We all enjoyed 10 nights of fun. We would eat together, enjoy the pool, go to the beach and Lenny would play music and we would have Bocci Tournaments. All the neighbors came and friends were invited. Everyone made something or brought something for dinner. Beemer was always a fan of Bennyfest. We brought him his towel and water bowl and he would hang out with Gizzy and run around with the kids.

When Bennyfest was over the next day or so Beemer was ready to run over to Sam's for more fun and ready to hang out again. "No party today Beem. Lenny went home." We would tell him. Beemer looked disappointed.

Beemer's Tale 308

Beemer waiting to go to Sam's

<u>Rob</u>

When Rob got remarried he was very busy with his new wife and her children. We did bring Beemer to Rob and his wife's new house for a visit. Beemer and their dog got along great. Beemer was so happy to see Rob.

We did not get to see Rob as often. We really missed seeing him. We love Rob and so glad he is happy. We are also very grateful as without Rob we would never have Beemer.

Chapter 19 – Therapy Visits – Part 2

Things have progressed from when Beemer first started being a Therapy Dog. Originally it was primarily Home Visits, Assisted Living Facilities and Nursing Homes. Now it has branched out to help so many others. Over the years we expanded our Pet Therapy Visits to include different places. It is a proven scientific fact that animals help calm people and lower blood pressure.

Not every dog is a match for Pet Therapy just like not every dog is a match as a Service Dog for the Blind and other Services. But if you think your pet may be a match then it is definitely worth considering. Also handlers have to be aware of the type of visits to attend. When going to hospitals and Assisted Living facilities there are people in all stages of health conditions. Many people are in wheel chairs, use canes, and have injuries. That may not be for everyone but the good news is that there are so many other venues for visits. You can take your dog to the library for Reading with the Dogs for children to help build their confidence and improve their reading skills. You can visit college campuses to help de-stress the college students at exam time. Plus it is a bonus to walk around on campus. You can take a trip to the airport to help calm the passengers while waiting for a flight and maybe even get vacation ideas. You can help give something back in return to our Military in helping them adjust and deal with PTSD upon returning from being overseas. Whatever your passion is go for it.

We need to recertify every year with the Pet Therapy Association and list all the places we had visited with Beemer.

Beemer's Tale 310

You have to submit a copy of their shots to make sure they are up-to-date and send a current picture to update your badge. Initially you had to send in a printed picture and then the Association went online so you could send via email. Even at the age of 10 Beemer got a message back with a compliment.

>**Sent:** Monday, November 07, 2011 7:12 PM
>**Subject:** Renewal Picture
>
>*Dear Agency,*
>
>>*Here is latest picture for Beemer. I have sent the application in the mail and asked the Vet to fax his shot records.*
>
>*Thank You,*
>*Louann*

>**Date:** Tuesday, November 08, 2011 3:17 PM
>**Subject:** RE: Renewal Picture
>
>*Thank you for the photo. He's very cute!*
>
>*Sue*

Over the years, Beemer did so many Pet Therapy visits there is no way to convey all of them. Each one was great in its own way and benefited all. The following is a summary of some of the more impacting ones.

<u>Neurological Unit</u>

> One day Katie called us. "A friend of mine is looking for some Pet Therapy dogs to come to the Neurological Unit. I cannot go at the designated time. It is once a month on Saturdays. Would you be interested? It is close by and only a ten minute drive. It is across the highway past the Bridge Park."
>
> "This sounds great for us. Thanks yes we would definitely be interested."
>
> "Great I will give you the contact information and you can call Pam. She is the Captain for that site."
>
> "Perfect. I will definitely call Pam."
>
> "Thanks so much for covering this one."
>
> "So glad we can make it."
>
> Katie referred us and gave us Pam's number. We called Pam. Pam was very nice; her Therapy Dog is a tan Pug named Lulu.

Beemer's Tale 312

Lulu

"We will meet you out front beforehand so Beemer and Lulu can get acquainted. " Pam suggested.

"Sounds great."

"Also I will send an email every month as a reminder."

"That would be great. Thanks so much. Looking forward to it. See you then."

We met outside 15 minutes before the designated time of the visit.

"Hi this is Beemer and this is my husband Jack."

"So nice to meet you. Hi Beemer. He is so cute. This is Lulu. Sometimes she can be a little shy of bigger dogs."

"Go easy Beem." Beemer went over to Lulu and gently sniffed. Lulu wasn't crazy about sniffing him back but was ok with him.

"Hey she is doing great so far." Pam said.

We let them walk around a little bit together.

"I think we are good and ready to go in." Pam said.

We walked into the recreation room which was set up with TV, tables, chairs and couches.

There were about 8 people sitting around the room. Pat introduced us and we told everyone about Beemer.

It was a great combination as some people loved smaller dogs and others loved bigger dogs. The first person to speak was Kevin. "I was hoping for a bigger dog to visit. Come here big guy." "Go say hi Beemer." Beemer went right over and Kevin hugged and petted him while Beemer was wagging his tail.

We brought Lulu and Beemer over to each person to see them.

After our first visit Pam asked "So what do you think?"

"I think it is terrific. We definitely will be back." I said.

"The people really seemed to enjoy it." Jack said.

"Yes they really do." Pam agreed. "Great. Maybe we can even meet at the park and have Lulu and Beemer socialize more. Would help Lulu get more familiar with being around bigger dogs."

"Sure. We take Beemer to the park down the street all the time."

"I'll email you to set it up and will definitely see you next month."

We thought it was so fitting; everyone remembered Beemer's name but not ours and that is how it should be. As soon as we pulled in the parking lot for our next visit and were getting out of the car we would hear "Beemer, Beemer!". The residents would call out his name and wave as they saw us walking in and they were heading toward the recreation room. It was such a great feeling to see how happy they were to see him and remember his name.

Jack called his friend Max who he used to work with. "Hey guess where we are doing Pet Therapy visits with Beemer?" Jack said to Max.

"Have no idea." Max replied.

"At your place on Saturdays."

"Really? I am sure the residents love it."

"Yeah it's great. We go once a month."

"Oh - I am only on call there on weekends in case something happens."

"Too bad we won't get to see you there."

"Well I'll let you know if I am ever there when you go."

"Cool."

Max is head of maintenance at the facility. He works full time Monday thru Friday.

After several visits we brought toys so the people could throw them and have Lulu and Beemer get them. I had to explain that Beemer never learned to 'Fetch' but if I went over and said 'Give' he would let me have it. It was a more confined space so I could get to him quicker. Everyone laughed and thought it was so funny. Lulu would chase the ball like crazy and then bring it back so someone could throw it again. Just hearing all the laughter; it was truly the best hour well spent every time we went.

Sleeping on the Job

>Since they had couches in the recreation room one visit Beemer decided to make himself at home and jumped on the couch. "No Beem this is not your couch. You need to get down." Everyone protested and said "Let him stay on the couch." I looked at Pam and she nodded. It became a thing where Beemer would lay on the couch and everyone took turns to sit by him and pet him.

>After running around with the toys Beemer hopped up on the couch and when one of the residents was petting him Beemer started to close his eyes. I said "Hey Beemer. No Sleeping on the Job. You can get fired." Everyone roared with laughter.

>– It then became our standing joke each visit if Beemer was on the couch and started to close his eyes I would say "No sleeping on the job."

We really connected at the Neurological Unit since we got to see the majority of the people who lived there consistently. With Assisted Living and Rehab people would come and go more often. Sometimes we would see the same people and they would remember Beemer, but not like at the Neurological Unit. There is a difference when you see someone once in awhile and when you see them consecutively every month for years. You develop a friendship over time.

We really got to know the people who lived there. You could not ask anyone details on their situation but over the years as they got to know us they would share. We really care about them. We looked forward to these visits to see how everyone was doing.

To see the progression over the years of the residents on our visits and the improvements in their health was amazing. We didn't do just one visit. It was years of visits where people counted on you coming.

Ron

>Our visits give Ron a purpose. He would walk in with his calendar book under his arm. He would write down the date of our next visit in his book to make sure everyone knew when we were coming. If there was a Holiday we would be moved to the following week. It is so thoughtful. Ron has a great mind and memory for dates and numbers.
>
>Ron loves Beemer. He wants to take Beemer's leash and be the one to walk him around the room to see everyone. Ron always offers to watch Beemer if we are going away. "Oh thank you so much that is so nice of you to offer." We knew it wasn't possible but thought it was so sweet and sincere of him to offer. He said it every time we came to visit.

Tom

The first visit Tom's hand was shaking so badly he could hardly even pet Beemer. His hand would just hover over Beemer trying to get close enough to touch him. God Bless Beemer as he never flinched. Most dogs I know that were not trained Therapy Dogs would jump off the couch or balk at the attempt to pet. Beemer was so patient as Tom tried to pet him. After two years Tom was able to run his hand smoothly down Beemer's back. It was awesome.

Tom was so happy. "He is so soft." he said. I had all I could do not to cry. Such a gift that we take for granted every day.

This reminded me of my Mom. Her hands also had a terrible shake where at one point she needed assistance to eat. When we came to visit she would make the effort to touch Beemer. The happiness of accomplishment in her determination to pet him calmly was indescribable.

Greg

Greg is an artist. He would do big posters and bring them in to show us. He dressed like a hippie back from the 70's but made it work for modern day. His artwork is astounding. He walks with a limp but would walk in proudly with his artwork under his arm. Greg did not come every time we were there so when he did come we were always glad to see him.

Dee

Dee has a job in a factory packing boxes. Dee has the greatest laugh. She would clap her hands and laugh so you couldn't help but laugh along with her. She is such a sweet person. Dee has a cat. "Whitey always sits in the window." Dee said. "That is great. Beemer is good friends with our neighbor's cat Jack. They say hello nose to nose and sit together when we have BBQs." Diane loved Beemer for that and gave him a big hug. "Maybe Whitey and Beemer can meet someday." "Maybe." I could not tell her no as we were not allowed in the resident's place and Whitey never went outside, but it made her happy to think about.

Kevin

Kevin is a jock at heart. Kevin is always encouraging others to go out back for a basketball game. Kevin is very cool. He loves Beemer as he prefers larger dogs. Kevin is a fan of comics and movies and loves to tell jokes. He has a joke for us every time we came. We would share stories of our favorite superheroes and what movies we saw. "Beemer is going to be Superman for Halloween this year." Jack said. "Beemer you will be a great Superman." Kevin replied.

Kevin knew all that was going on in the facility and is very versed in current events. He would tell you straight-out.

Singing to the Dogs – Sophie

Sophie loves to sing. She is always singing or humming. She has fiery red hair. Sophie's preference was small dogs so she loved Lulu. Sophie would sit on the couch with Lulu on her lap and sing her a song. Sophie was no Taylor Swift but she could carry a tune. Beemer would be on the other end of the couch. Sophie would sing to the dogs and it was so sweet everyone would patiently let her entertain us. We all clapped when Sophie finished.

Mark

Mark came across as rough and tough but had a soft spot for dogs. He has a lot of really colorful tattoos. He sat back in the corner and did not really interact with the others but enjoyed the visits. Mark would call the dogs over to where he was and would pet them as they came over. On a few occasions we had a conversation. We told him how we got Beemer and how he was a rescue from the shelter. "I would have a dog of my own if I could." "Well maybe someday you will." I said. I saw him one time kiss Beemer on his head.

Get Some Fresh Air

On a few occasions when it was really nice outside we went out back behind the recreation room where they had a patio and picnic tables. We did our Pet Therapy Visit outside. It was great as they could see Lulu and Beemer run around on the grass. Kevin got to throw the ball farther than inside and loved to see Beemer take off. "Wow he is really fast like 'The Flash'." I smiled "Yes he is." Everyone loved it. It was so wonderful to hear their laughter and to forget their troubles even for just an hour.

After a number of visits Lulu became friends with Beemer and was happy to see him. "I can't believe how well she has done with Beemer." Pam would say.

"I am so glad. Beemer loves everybody."

"Yes that definitely shows." Now we can add Lulu to Beemer's Buddies list.

Pam had lined up some other folks to come and join us. Sometimes Dakota, a beautiful Husky with blue eyes, and his handler Paul would come but not every time. Also sometimes Jan would come with her white miniature poodle Cuddles.

Get Well

In the second year of our visits Lulu had to have a small procedure done. Beemer and I had to hold down the fort as Pat and Lulu could not attend. Sometimes either Dakota and Paul or Jan and Cuddles would come but not every time. Beemer, Jack and I were always there.

Jack had a great idea. "I think we should get a Get Well card for everyone to sign to send to Lulu."

Jack brought a pack of colored pens. With pens in hand Jack walked around to everyone to let them sign the card and pick the color pen they wanted to use to sign. If someone could not sign then we asked what they would like to say and we wrote it for them and showed them so they could see their name and message that was included in the card.

Sophie said "I want Lulu to feel better since she makes us feel better." That really touched my heart. "I know Lulu and Pam will really appreciate that." I said. "And when Lulu is back you can sing her a song."

It really meant a lot to them to be able to sign their names and send Get Well wishes to Lulu. Every time we came they asked how she was doing and when Lulu would be back. "She is doing great and hopefully Lulu will be back next month."

After our visit at the Neurological Unit we always took Beemer to the Bridge Park as a reward. It was on our way home and it was his time to let loose in the park after working.

Personally I loved going to the Neurological Unit; it was one of my favorite visits. We felt that Beemer had a connection with everyone there and really helped them.

When the Neurological Unit changed management they started scheduling outings and off site therapy for the residents. We were sad to see our time end there. We wished everyone well. We sometimes see some of the residents we used to visit out shopping with their aids. We would ask how they were doing and mentioned "Beemer" so they would remember who we were. "How's he doing?"

"He's great – he's home sleeping on the couch just like on our visits." That got a laugh.

"Tell him I said hi."

"Will do. So good to see you."

Teenager Rehabilitation

One of the people we went to Pet Therapy training with, Joey, had told us about visiting a Rehabilitation Facility for teenagers. She went with her Sassy. Beemer loves kids so we thought that sounded interesting. We asked her for the information and it was about 40 minutes from where we lived. We decided to take Beemer and try it. We were instructed to not ask anything specific on their condition on our visits. If someone said something we could respond positively to what they told us. The Pet Therapy visits were a reward for them based on their progress.

The first time we went to the Rehabilitation Facility we all gathered in the parking lot. When it was our time to go in we all had to go in the back door. There were a lot of Pet Therapy dogs who came to this visit. There were 15 Therapy Dogs that day. We all had to go up 2 flights of stairs to get to the room where they held the visits. While walking up the stairs it hit me that this is amazing. Here we have 15 dogs and handlers walking together and none of the dogs were barking. No one went off track. Everyone was just walking side by side in unison just as they were trained to do.

Once inside the room we would line up along the wall.

You had to write a bio about your Therapy Dog to tell the teenagers something about them. You also would show them a few tricks that they can do. Each person got up and took a turn. Once everyone was done then we spread out around the room so the teenagers could freely come over and visit hands on with the dogs.

Beemer's Bio

>Beemer was found by the side of the road with a broken leg. He was rescued from the shelter and became a Therapy Dog.
>
>Beemer learned to give paw early on since he loved Ham. [I held out my hand and Beemer demonstrated.]
>
>We graduated to sitting up. [I waved my hand up and Beemer sat up. I gave him a treat.]
>
>We also taught him to do a circle. [I pointed my index finger down and moved it in a circle and Beemer turned around in a circle.]
>
>Beemer loves to run and does Agility. [I stood with legs apart and pointed and Beemer did a Figure 8 around my legs and he got another treat.]
>
>Can anyone guess what kind of dog Beemer is? [Some would shout out 'Lab', 'Boxer', 'Pit']
>
>Beemer is a Lab/Pit Mix.
>
>Here are some fun facts about Pit Bulls.

Beemer's Tale

They were once considered one of America's Favorite Breeds. All of the following were Pit Bulls.

- Petey from the Little Rascals
- The RCA Dog Nipper
- The Buster Brown Shoe Mascot Tige

Even the Army used a Pit Bull as a Mascot. World War I posters had them as a symbol for the United States as they were respected for their Loyalty, Determination and Bravery.

- One of the most decorated dogs to serve in the military was Sergeant Stubby who was a Pit Bull type. He served with soldiers in World War I and was awarded the Purple Heart.

Beemer loves all people and all animals. He is even friends with our neighbor's cat Jack who looks like Garfield. And Jack loves to eat.

Beemer loves to go to the beach and to the park. When he gets home he is a couch potato.

Thank You for having us.

I thought it would be fun for the kids to see Beemer do a bit of Agility so we worked on his new trick. I would stand tall with feet apart and Beemer would do a Figure 8 around my legs similar to the weave poles in Agility. They all loved that one.

The teens really were so happy seeing and visiting with all the dogs. They missed their pets at home. They would gravitate to the dog that was similar to their own pet or one breed that they liked. Many came to see Beemer as he was very different. He was the only Lab/Pit Bull mix. Many were pure breeds including German Shepherd, Golden Retriever, and Basset Hound.

Here is an email excerpt from our Captain after our visit.

Date: Sunday, November 15, 2009 18:25

Subject: thank you

"15 therapy dogs and their handlers - willing to give up their afternoon to make someone else's day better

35 teenagers singing God Bless America along with a basset hound,
a delightful indoor Frisbee trick demonstration- handlers telling stories and answering questions about their German Shepherds, pit mix, Portuguese water dog, labradoodle, goldens, border collies, old english sheep dog, delightful mutts and great danes
All in one room - not one growl, not one misbehavior- impressive - a credit to their handlers ......

I started to count smiles (kids) got to 45 before I lost count and we were not even half way done with our visit.
A staff member stopped me today and said "This is our favorite day of the month (when the dogs come out)."
.....I wanted everyone to know I looked around the room today and I think each one of you and your dog- is something special"

Beemer's Tale 326

There is no better reward.

One day Jack was walking Beemer and on his way home from the Dock he came across four teenagers sitting at the corner. As he walked by they said "He is so beautiful. What is his name?" Jack stopped to let them pet him. "Beemer." Jack replied. "He is a rescue from the shelter and he is a Therapy Dog. He visits patients in hospitals and even visits the Teenagers in the Rehabilitation Facility 40 minutes north of here." The one girl said "OMG. I know someone who was there. Hold on." She whipped out her phone and made a call. "Hi. Guess who I am with right now? I am with Beemer who visits where you were. Yeah he is black with white feet. Yes. He is so cool. I'll call you later. Bye." As she hung up she turned to Jack and explained how her friend was there and her friend remembered Beemer.

It was a funny coincidence. That was after the first time we took Beemer to visit the Teenager Rehab Facility. Neither one of us ever saw those teenagers who were down at the corner that day again. We took it as a sign that it was positive and Beemer was doing good work. We continued to go to the Teen Rehab. We went every time we were available.

<u>One on One</u>

One girl came over and sat on the floor next to Beemer with her legs folded like a pretzel. She started to cry. "Are you okay?" I asked. "Yes. Just missing my two dogs at home." "Aww what kind are they?" "They are pit bulls just like him." She hugged Beemer. "I am sure they miss you too. What are their names?" "Coco and Bailey. I love them so much." My heart immediately went out to her. "Well hopefully you will see them soon." I always tried to be positive and if appropriate add a little humor. "Thank you for coming here." She said. "We are glad to be here. Beemer loves to visit. Plus all the hugs." She laughed at that and gave him another.

On another visit a boy came over and sat in a chair next to us. "Hi. This is Beemer. What is your name?" "I'm Ben." "Hi Ben. Do you have any pets?" "No." "Do you have any hobbies?" "I like to play music." "Really? Beemer loves music." Ben perked up. "What instrument do you play?" "I play the piano." "Oh wow that is so great. I always wished I stayed with taking lessons. You definitely should stay with it." "Yeah I really like it." "You definitely can do it." He stood up and pet Beemer's head and said "Bye." "Bye. Nice to meet you Ben." I hope Ben sticks with the music. Jack and I have such an admiration for anyone who can play music or sing. It is another kind of gift.

Sometimes we would have a number of teens at the same time sitting around Beemer petting him and talking. It reminded me of when the high school students at Rob's would sit around and visit with Beemer.

The Captain of our visits said it best – nothing better than to try to make someone else feel better.

Wish we could have gone more often to Pet Therapy visits, but because of my work we were limited. We did go every chance we could. The local paper had a weekly picture of the Therapy Dog visits during the week at Assisted Living or for Reading to the Dogs at the Library. Our friend Katie went to all those events.

We would always see her picture with Misty. Katie had the most beautiful outfits for herself and Misty. They were so elaborate and festive. You could not help but smile when seeing them together. It would have been great if we could have joined them. "You go Katie and Misty!" we said whenever we saw their picture.

Misty enjoying a Boat Ride

Dog Walk for Cancer

In 2011 they relocated the Dog Walk for Cancer event from the County Park to the Local Baseball Stadium.

I remember the first time we went at the Stadium. "You are going to the Baseball Stadium Beem. Hot Dog!"

It was really a very nice location. They set up an Agility Demonstration and a Pet Adoption Promotion. There was a blessing for the dogs at every event and an auction for donations to win prizes. We always saw Beemer's trainers from his school as they had a booth set up at the event. We saw Katie and Misty there too many times and others we met from going every year. People of all ages and children and lots of dogs would attend. Even people without dogs would come. It was a great day for a great cause.

Beemer with Paul his trainer at the Dog Walk for Cancer

Assisted Living Facilities and Home Visits

Our neighbor Sheila had a fall and went to the hospital. She was then transferred to a Rehab Facility until she could get back on her feet. The first time Jack and I went to visit her we were not sure how she was doing so we did not bring Beemer. Instead we brought a picture of her dog Babe with Beemer down at the Dock when we had minded Babe. "Oh I love this." Sheila said. "Can you put it up on my bulletin board so I can see it every day?" Sheila told us the picture inspired so many conversations with the aids and people who came to visit. Beemer did a Pet Therapy visit via his picture.

Beemer and Babe at the Dock

We continued our Assisted Living and Home Visits whenever we were available. Definitely at Holiday time. One of the aids told us that many residents go in the designated room an hour earlier than we are scheduled to visit as they do not want to miss it.

Seniors have one of the highest rates for loneliness. Many live alone and sadly often wait for the mail carrier as that may be the only person they see or can talk to that day. We felt our Home Visits with Beemer were so important to family, friends and neighbors who could not get out of the house.

Shades of Grey

> I actually looked it up and both spellings of grey and gray are correct. The guideline is grAy is how it is spelled in America and grEy is how it is spelled in England.
>
> Up until Beemer was 13 no one could believe his age and how old he was.
>
> "How old is he?"
>
> "Beemer is my teenager; he is 13."
>
> "Really? He looks so much younger." Or "I would never have guessed."
>
> When people said "Wow he is in such good shape. You took really good care of him."
>
> Our reply was "Thank you. We try. We always give him good food and take him to walk every day. We take him almost every day to walk to keep in shape."
>
> "You can only tell he is a little older from the gray."
>
> "Yes he is distinguished."

Beemer's Tale

The ladies at the Assisted Living Facilities would call Beemer "Sugar Puss." I thought that was such a 'sweet' way of saying he was getting a little older. As he continued to get more gray after 13 people would ask his age and say he looked like a senior. I always corrected them and said "No - he is my teenager and we keep him going every day!"

Beemer was never overweight. We really did try to keep him in good shape with food and exercise. Before we moved to Gerry's house Beemer was going to Agility which was indoors so he got extra exercise on weekends if the weather was not good. We always walked as long as the weather allowed. Once we moved across the street, if the weather was bad our new house is set up with an open floor plan so you can actually do a circle within the house. The kids love it when they come and run around and around. It gave me the idea to do laps with Beemer like we are on a track. So every time it was too cold, snowy or raining we did our laps at night inside.

I would always sing songs as we made our laps. "This is how we do it" or "Everything is awesome" or "Exercise exercise come 'on everybody do your exercise."

Gift of Giving

Pets on any level are a gift. You have to admire what they contribute to your life. Service dogs for the blind, deaf or other disability are incomparable to what they provide to enhance others' lives. You see the stories on TV or read about it on the internet. The stories are so overwhelming and heartwarming. They save lives. They improve people's health. Pet Therapy for those who do not or cannot have pets also gives to others. I am so grateful that we are able to be a part of that gift.

Without a doubt it is definitely right for Beemer and I to do Pet Therapy. There are so many people who can benefit. Beemer has touched hundreds of people over the years. From personal experience I can say if you do decide to do Pet Therapy it is worth every second of making someone else feel better even for a moment.

Chapter 20 – Holistic Healing and Medication

<u>2014 Operation</u>

Beemer had developed a small cyst under his left front leg. Over time it got larger. The Vet said it was not harming him or cancerous thankfully but if it got much larger it could affect his walking. We were leery of putting Beemer under anesthesia and to have him go through an operation but we thought overall it was for the best.

When we came to pick him up he was still a little groggy. I kneeled down to greet him as he came out. "Hi my Beauty. How you doing?" I gently petted him.

"Hi ya Beem." Jack said. It was so hard to see him like that but we think he was happy we were there to take him home. "You are going home Beem." I said.

As the night went on Beemer just could not get comfortable. Just like in people things that bother us always seem worse at night. It was the only time Beemer ever cried out from pain. We felt terrible. We gave him his pain pill and tried to comfort him. We played calming music. We finally got him to settle down. He just wanted to keep going outside and we kept saying "Beem you have to rest my boy." We didn't want him to put extra stress on the stitches. After two days he was much better thankfully. After two weeks he got his stitches out and was as good as new.

At that time the Vet also mentioned Beemer was starting to get Arthritis in his back legs. He suggested giving him an aspirin at night to help with sleeping even after he healed from the operation.

We had a very hard time giving Beemer his aspirin. I looked up online and they said that the particular medication he is on is very bitter tasting. We never wanted to put the pills in his food so he would stop eating his food if he found a pill. We put his allergy pill in slices of cheese and that worked great for years. I called it his "Aftertizer" or "Lagnaippe – a little something extra" after he ate his food. When we tried it with the aspirin he kept spitting them out. We then tried hot dogs and breakfast sausages as they are easy to hide the pills in. These also worked great for a while. Next we tried Cream Puffs which became "Here's dessert!" after eating his dinner. All these worked for a while but the aspirin was so bitter he found it.

I googled online to see if there were any tricks. One suggestion was to get empty gel capsules and put the pills in there and then they won't taste it. "Hey Jack look at this. That's a great idea! I am definitely going to try that." The next day I went to the Pharmacy.

When it was my turn I walked up the counter. "Hi I was wondering if you sell empty capsules."

"Empty?"

"Yes I... well let me be honest." The pharmacist tilted her head and looked like she was waiting for a crazy story.

"I need to give pills to my dog and they are really bitter so he either won't take them or spits them out. I wanted to put them in the capsules."

"Oh ok sounds like it would work. Let me see what I have in the back."

She brought back a small box. "How are these? Do they look big enough?"

I looked in the box. "Yes I think they will work. Great – thank you so much. I really appreciate it."

"No problem." She rang it up and I paid. "Thanks so much again."

"Good luck."

"Thanks."

Not sure she believed me, but I was grateful she found something.

The pills did not fit in the capsules whole so we had to cut them in half. I felt like the pharmacist with the pill cutter and loading pills in the capsules. It worked like a charm so it was worth it.

The next time I went back for a refill for more capsules I said "These worked perfectly. It made it so much easier giving Beemer his pills."

"I am glad it worked."

"Me too."

Coconut Oil

When we brought Beemer back to have his stitches out we noticed he had a little rash on his back leg. The Vet suggested putting on a warm compress and then putting a little coconut oil on it. Beemer loved the warm compress. "Hey Beem. People pay big money for this in the spa." I would then put a little coconut oil on his front leg before the back one as it smelled so good he wanted to lick it and it was perfectly safe for him. There was even nutritional value. This way Beemer would lick the front leg and leave the back one alone. It was amazing but the next day it looked better and the second day the rash was gone. I think I am going to put coconut oil on everything.

Sundown

After Beemer's 13th Birthday he started getting anxious at night. He was fine during the day but at bedtime or during the night he would pant and walk around. We took him to the Vet and they thought it was from him being uncomfortable from the arthritis in his back legs. They suggested increasing his pain medication at night to see if it eased the symptoms and to massage his back legs.

In addition to the pain medication we tried Holistic Healing options. We would play calming music; the Sounds of the Seasons from the Cable Channel to have a Zen effect. We tried Aromatherapy with a calming spray we would spray on the couch and the bed. We took him for Reiki and Massages. We wanted to try everything to make him feel better. The Reiki and Massage actually did help his back legs. After taking him for several sessions we continued to massage his back legs on our own.

Beemer was better most nights but still on occasion get up and walk around sometimes. On our next Vet visit they recommended a milk based product. It was like giving a child warm milk at night to help them sleep. That made a world of difference. Finally everyone got a good night's sleep all night long.

A year later Beemer's pacing at night started up again. Back to the Vet we went and they said since he is getting older the Arthritis is more impacting. They suggested giving him something to relax him that would be stronger than the milk based product we had been giving him. We really were very unhappy to have to give him another medication and yet we did not want him to be in any kind of pain so we tried it. At first it did not seem to do anything but after a week he was better. He was eating and drinking and sleeping like he always did.

Alternatives

We are always open to alternative treatments. Based on suggestions from Beemer's Doctors we also looked into Laser Light Therapy, Acupuncture and Swimming Therapy. Just like for people there are so many options available for animals.

Because Beemer was not a fan of the water we knew he would not like Swimming Therapy so we ruled that one out, but Acupuncture may definitely be a possibility.

We also made sure we were giving him good quality food.

Hot to Trot

Beemer always loved to run. It was a joy to watch him. Whenever you told Beemer to 'Come' he would either run up to you and stop short right in front of you or if he was going too fast he would whiz by and circle back around.

Now that Beemer is older he did not run around with the intensity of his younger years. I still kneel down and open my arms like we did at school. Beemer does more of a trot than a run but he still does it to his best excitedly. He comes into my arms for a big hug and kiss. Priceless.

Back to Where He Started

After Beemer's operation Jack thought it was better to put a gate up across the garage for Beemer's protection. He is so friendly and in case any other dogs would come to play we did not want to take the chance that they would jump on him or hurt Beemer if he was out on the front lawn. When my sister's dogs came the last few times Beemer would try to run too much with them and then take a day or two to recover. We put a bed down for him to lay on in front of the gate so he could see out and we would sit in the garage on nice days. I felt sad to see him looking out the gate as that was his view when he was in the shelter – looking out behind bars. Especially since prior to his operation Beemer would sit out on the front lawn and never leave the property. He got so many compliments as people and children passed by.

Luckily though Beemer still got visitors and kudos. Our friend Kasey from around the block always stops by to see Beemer with her Dudley if we are outside. With tails wagging Beemer on the inside of the gate and Dudley on the outside they would say hello. Kasey pets Beemer on the head. "He is such a sweet boy." I smiled "Thanks yes he really is. And Dudley's a good boy too. Right Dudley?" Dudley's whole back end would wag as I pet him over the gate.

Beemer's biggest fan Winston also always comes by to see Beemer when Annie and Don walk him down the street. "Winston tries to come up the driveway every time we pass by even if the garage door is not open." Annie said. "Aww Winston we are always so happy to see you." I reached through the gate to pet him. Beemer and Winston would sniff with tails wagging on opposite sides of the gate. "Hi Beemer. How are you doing?" Annie asked. "He's doing well as you can see wagging away." "Beemer you just made Winston's day!"

Adjustments

The next year we could see a difference in Beemer's back legs. Beemer's front legs were strong but from the arthritis in his back legs, jumping was getting harder for Beemer. He had some misses trying to jump on the couch, the bed and in the car. "Oww Beem are you okay?" We would go right over and inspect and massage him. We did not want him to hurt himself. It hurt us in a different way. It was like a stab in the gut. Especially since he always jumped so high and so far his whole life and when he was doing Agility. We did not want to think of it as Beemer was getting older. I said "Beem you are my 'Spring Chicken.'"

I researched online and in catalogs and we got Beemer a portable Ramp. It is fantastic. It was very lightweight and folded in half. It could hold up to 300 pounds so we knew it was not a problem for Beemer who was always between 50 and 60 lbs. We used it for everything. It made it safer and easier for Beemer to walk up versus trying to jump.

One lady at the park stopped to pet Beemer. "How old is he?" she asked.

"He is my teenager. He is 14" I said with a smile.

"He is still so handsome and very sweet."

"Thank you. Yes he is."

When we were leaving the same lady from earlier saw us putting up Beemer's ramp to get in the car. "Aww you are such a good Mommy!"

I pointed to the ramp. "This is priceless since it's hard to jump in, this way we can keep him going."

"That's excellent."

We could see Beemer's frustration as he wanted to jump on the couch himself. He always prided himself on doing things himself. We measured and the couch was 20 inches high. He would walk around the coffee table a number of times before trying to jump on. Jack tried to remove the legs to the couch to lower it but it was constructed so that was not an option. We decided to also use the ramp to let Beemer walk right up to lay on the couch. On good days he could jump up himself. On not so good days we would set up the ramp so he could walk up. It was difficult for Beemer to lay on the floor with his arthritis. It was hard for him to lay down and then get up from the hardwood floor. It was much better for him to be on the couch. Plus this was always how he had lived. Beemer is a couch potato until it is time for walks, activities, meals or work.

Bed Ritual

When it was time for bed I would always say "It's time for the big jumbo." As I patted the bed. Beemer would come and jump up on the bed. Didn't realize it was so high 25" inches. He did it so effortlessly for 8 years.

When he started having issues with his back legs we had a new bed ritual. After Beemer's last time outside for the night we would set the ramp up and Beemer could walk right up on the bed. He could jump off no problem as he landed on his front legs which were stronger. Jumping up using his back legs was more difficult. Beemer had no problem walking up the ramp to bed. Beemer had to take his last pill of the day, his aspirin, so he could sleep better. If he would not take it with dinner then sometimes we would have a 'Picnic in Bed.' I would bring all kinds of treats or snacks so he could get his pill. Sometimes I would join him in having a late night treat.

I would massage his back and legs and say "Sleep Well Heal Well, Feel Well Be Well."

After 6 months we thought it was too much pressure on his back legs to jump off. Sometimes he would hesitate and we would help him off. We decided to lower the bed. Jack took off the platform and lowered the bed by 5 inches. That was better for a while. Then we removed the box spring, another 9 inches, so it was only the mattress on the floor. This way he could just step up on the bed. Beemer was so happy he could just walk on by himself anytime he wanted. Sometimes he would hang out on the bed while Jack or I were getting changed. I joked with all my family and friends.

"Hey come on back and see our Hippie Bed." They would walk into our bedroom and laugh.

"You can sleep like that?"

"Actually it is not that bad. The mattress is really comfortable."

I really did feel like a hippie back from the 70's like you would see on the news or in old movies with the mattress on the floor, but it was totally worth it as it gave Beemer the ease to do it himself. It gave him back some of his independence in case he wanted to go there at any time and not just for bedtime.

What we do for our loved ones - little adjustments that are worth a King's Ransom and Beemer is the King.

Hugs

There is nothing better than hugs with the Beem. Sitting on the couch hugging the Beem definitely makes my day. Big hugs at bedtime and then seeing him stretch out on the bed.

Because of Beemer's arthritis we started to have to help him up the stairs. I had looked up some aids they have available to help you walk your dog up stairs safely. There were so many to choose from. I spoke with my friend Karen to see if she knew of one's people may have recommended since she worked with the Bulldog Rescue. She sent us a link and we purchased a GingerLead which is a support around Beemer's tummy with handles.

It works great. Jack would use the lead. He would use one hand to help lift Beemer up the stairs. It was too hard for me to do one handed. Instead I would help him up wheel barrel style so I could get a better grip using two hands. Before we went up I would hug him.

"Hugs for my love bug." I would say and kiss him on his head 3 times. "Ready Beem?" I would sing "We do it together. We do it together." I would have his back end and he would make his way up with his front legs. Once we made it to the top step I would say "One more and we're in the door."

Prayers

In our backyard we have a statue of St. Frances on a pedestal. He stands in front of a trellis covered in ivy with a lantern hanging overhead. Every morning Beemer would stand in the sun in front of St. Francis as if to say 'Good Morning.'

Gerry had put it there when she lived here with her parents. It seemed to fit and we wanted to leave it in honor. It was funny that Gerry's Dad's name was Francis and my Grandfather's name was Francis. They both were always called Frank. They are in good company with St. Francis.

When Beemer didn't feel well I offered up many prayers to St. Francis. "Please help my Beemer to feel well." When he had a good day I was so grateful. When Beemer didn't have a good day I would say "Sorry Beem. I guess St. Francis was busy today. Hopefully he will be by tomorrow."

Chapter 21 – Food – The Enemy

We still had to be creative in finding ideas to give Beemer his medication. Even though we had the capsules sometimes he would bite into whatever we put them in and once he found it forget it. We tried all kinds of things including steak, roast beef with gravy, salami, pulled pork, hot dogs, and meatballs. Anything we thought we could hide pills in. Online they say sometimes they pick up signals depending on how you are giving it to them. If you are anxious about it they can sense it and Beemer was always in tune to how people were feeling. I would try to get excited about it as if it was a really special snack. We would change it up so he would not catch on or so we thought but his nose always knows. He would always smell what we brought. Sometimes it worked well and others not, but we kept trying.

Beemer started to lose interest in his dog food. He usually ate in the morning but at dinner time he would either eat a little bit or leave it. We added extra meat and leftovers we had to make it more enticing but he definitely was not digging it.

The problem with that is if he does not eat his food then we could not give him his pills. It was recommended that the pills be given with food. "What's the matter my boy – you don't like it? You want something else?" It was upsetting as you wanted him to eat. Just like with children you offer and try different things just so they will eat something. Sometimes he would eat and then go outside and throw up. "Oh no! Now he lost his pills." I said to Jack.

Beemer's Tale 348

We really did not know what was going on as previously Beemer always loved all food and sharing meals. We were concerned that Beemer would not get his medication so we called the Vet to ask for suggestions.

"It would be good to try some ground meat with rice and maybe think about giving him wet dog food instead of dry."

"That sounds good. We will definitely try it."

"Is he drinking enough water as it is important that he does not get dehydrated?"

"Yes he drinks water no problem. It is just the food where he is not interested."

"Let us know how he is doing."

"Thanks so much. We will."

Jack cooked ground meat or salmon with rice to try to get Beemer to eat.

Mission

I was on a mission. I wanted to get Beemer good food so he would eat and make him feel better. For food options I even typed in "How to get your dog to eat" on the internet. It was amazing they had so many great ideas. One valuable suggestion was to warm the food before you serve. This way it was more fragrant to help entice them to eat. We did that for Beemer anyway. We would warm any leftovers we had and put it on top of his dry dog food.

The internet suggested several brands of dog food which had a good smell to help them want to eat. I went to two local dog food stores to look for the brands that were recommended. I checked the ingredients on the brands and they all had great ingredients. They had a very minimal number of ingredients, primarily just protein and vitamins. I spoke with the owner of the store closest to our house. They had a Holistic dog food section. I bought five different kinds for Beemer to try.

After a few tries we did finally find one that Beemer liked. "Yay my boy! You have to eat to stay strong my Beauty."

Because we were giving him more protein we looked for ways to add fiber. We cooked Quinoa and added it to the wet food. I bought Sugar Free Oatmeal Cookies for dessert or treats. He actually loved them. Sugar Free has come a long way since my Grandmother who had Diabetes and had to eat only Sugar Free. The cookies she used to get were horrible. She would try to share them with my sister and I, but they were so awful you would rather not even have dessert. The new ones we got for Beemer were delicious. Jack and I would eat them right along with Beemer. I also got Beemer frozen yogurt for a special treat.

On occasion Beemer would still go outside and throw up after eating. We called the Vet and they suggested a nausea medication. "Oh boy another pill." I said to Jack. We felt bad for Beemer as we know how hard it was for him to take his pills. We tried it and luckily it definitely helped. We were just so happy Beemer was eating again.

After several months it was hit or miss on eating so we introduced other things to supplement. We noticed Beemer lost some weight. If he would not eat his dog food or the meals Jack cooked I got him a McDonald's Quarter Pounder with Cheese which was his favorite just like when we went together sometimes on the weekends. I served him his Quarter Pounder with cheese cut up small with no roll and would sing "You deserve a break today from McDonald's, from McDonald's."

Another good suggestion from the Vet was to try baby food as it was soft. I got him the beef and sweet potatoes. He seemed to like it. "There you go Beemy my boy." One of the Techs who we know so well Lynn was so sincere and sympathetic. She even offered to cook for Beemer. "I can make him one of my dishes I make for my dog when she is not feeling well." "Aww thank you so much. That is so truly nice of you to offer." We were so touched.

We cooked Beemer Bacon. No better smell than Bacon. He definitely loved that. Another favorite was Salmon Teriyaki from the Japanese place. We laughed saying he was on a pure protein low carb diet. Meat, Meat and Meat. We made him breakfast sausages, pork chops, hot dogs and macaroni and cheese. All the things kids loved he loved. Beemer really is our kid.

We even went to the local butcher where Paul and Diana's son Mick worked. They sell prepared foods also. Every time we came in Mick asked "How's Beemer?" Mick knew Beemer from living on the block. "He is hanging in thanks. How is Miss Hunter doing?" "She's good." "Excellent. We are here to get Beemer something good to eat. What's the special today?" Mick would suggest different items and we would get what we thought Beemer might like.

We call it "Little Victories" every time we tried something and Beemer liked it. His new favorite is mashed potatoes and Swedish Meatballs; they are easy on the belly and easy to eat.

Roller Coaster

I would talk to friends and family about how Beemer was not eating as he should.

"How's Beemer?" everyone asks. They know he is like my child.

"One day we are up and one day we are down. It's like a Roller Coaster."

I was going away with my sister to Atlantic City and we cut down our stay from two nights to one so I would not be away from Beemer too long.

Some people have the view "Are you crazy? He is just a dog!" I want to yell and scream like a crazy person but I don't. Instead I just say "Not to me. He is very special." I even call him my four-legged guy versus a dog. There are some pets who are just pets and they are special in their own way and then there are others who have a little extra something that makes them stand out and have a more human-like quality. They sense things and can relate to others more than just running after a ball. They save their owners, they sniff out cancer, they find survivors, and they comfort others. They are the four-legged heroes. Beemer is one of them.

I was telling a friend that I felt bad for having to shorten my trip but had to be there for Beemer. They turned to me and said "Never apologize for loving him like that." That really touched my heart. I actually had tears in my eyes as they totally understood how important he is to me and how much I love him.

Beemer's Tale 352

Chapter 22 – Last Leg

All the Techs and Doctors at our Vet love Beemer. When he was thirteen he had to get his Rabies shot. The shot was good for 3 years now versus every year when we started. Beemer's Doctor Dr. M. said "I want to see you and give you your next one in 3 years my man." That made us smile.

Most animals do not like going to the Vet. It is a high anxiety situation for them. Beemer is always calm when we go as is his nature. He knows all of them as extended family and friends who are there to help him be and feel better. It is a gift to find so many caring people that you feel so confident with to take care of your loved one.

A week before his 15th birthday Beemer stopped eating.

We did not know what he was feeling. He did not seem to be in pain in any way. Whenever we tried to give him something he would just smell it and put his head back down. "What's the matter my Beauty? Not hungry? I wish you could tell us." I just pet him gently.

Beemer would not eat anything. We tried everything and I mean we tried everything. We cooked and prepared and brought plate after plate of food to encourage him. We presented all kinds of concoctions and anything we could think of he might like out of desperation. We continued from morning till bedtime. The list included more baby food, ground beef, steak, salmon, rice, and even McDonald's. We knew we were in trouble when he would not eat McDonald's.

Beemer's Tale

Beemer would only drink water. It was a big concern as if he did not eat we could not give him his meds on an empty stomach. Because Beemer was not eating and only drinking water he would go out fairly often. Beemer would go outside and look around and up at the sky. Jack said "E.T.'s back. He is waiting for his spaceship." For some reason I did not find it funny. "Stop Jack." I said. But then I thought about it and that would be such a gift if someone or something could come and heal him like in the movie.

"Well if he does not eat by tomorrow morning I am calling the Vet." I said to Jack.

"Maybe he just has a 24 hour bug like people get." Jack said.

"I really hope so."

The next morning it was the same, Beemer would not eat. We could not entice Beemer with anything. We called the Vet in a panic. We brought him in and they did blood work and ran some tests. When the test results came back it turned out Beemer has Pancreatitis. The recommendation was for Beemer to go in the hospital to be on IV fluids until he could get back to a point of eating again. We were so torn at the thought of sending him back to being caged like when he was little in a shelter environment, but we had to try for his sake.

<u>Gilbert the Cat</u>

Our Vet has a Therapy Cat. His name is Gilbert. He is so cute. He is black with beautiful green eyes. We had never seen him before until Beemer went for his hospital stay. Gilbert stayed in the back as it was so busy in the waiting room and was only let out at the end of the day. He greeted us as we walked in to drop Beemer off. Jack is allergic and we laugh that all cats know and immediately go up to him. He came over to us and Beemer. Gilbert was so affectionate. Beemer and Gilbert sniffed nose to nose and were immediate friends. Gilbert is small and walked with a slight limp like Beemer did sometimes. I gave Gilbert a massage like I did for Beemer along his back and down his back legs.

"Does that feel good Gilbert? You are so handsome." He stretched his back legs out just like Beemer did. Even though Jack was allergic he bent down to pet Gilbert. Gilbert followed us to the back with Beemer. It broke my heart to have to see Beemer put in a cage since he had to be hooked up to an IV.

"We'll be back tomorrow Beemer to see you. You get better my Beauty – that is your job now my boy." I said.

"You get better so you can come home." Jack said with tears in his eyes.

I did my mantra that I did every night with Beemer "Sleep Well Heal Well Feel Well Be Well. We love you." We gave him hugs and kisses.

Once in the cage Gilbert came over and sat next to Beemer. They sniffed nose to nose again through the gate of the cage. I pet Gilbert on his head. "Gilbert please watch over our Beemer. Thank you." When we had to leave, Gilbert was still sitting next to Beemer. We cried all the way home.

Beemer's Tale 356

Gilbert

We went to see Beemer every day and take him out for a walk. We wanted to make sure he knew we were not leaving him there. It was heartbreaking to see him in a cage with an IV in his leg. Everyone was so supportive. They even let us come on Sunday when they were closed so we could come to see him. That meant so much to us.

Everyone really got to know him at the Vet since he was there every day. "He really is so sweet and such a good boy."

"Thank you so much for all you are doing for him. He really is. We are so lucky and blessed."

When the neighbors did not see us on our daily walks they came over and said. "Hey how are you guys doing? We haven't seen you."

"Beemer is in the hospital." Jack said.

"Oh no is he ok?"

"He has Pancreatitis and they are treating him."

"Well we really hope he will be ok and come home soon. We miss seeing you guys."

"Me too. We really want him home."

When others would ask we would say "We go to see him every day and he is hangin in."

"That is so good – wishing him the best."

"Us too. Thank you."

Family and friends would call and all asked how Beemer was doing. We are so appreciative that everyone cares so much. They all said "We are rooting for him." Or "He is in our prayers."

"Aww - Thank you. Thank you so much." We could not have asked for more support.

Beemer was in the hospital for his 15th birthday so we brought in a special tray of cookies for everyone to enjoy and celebrate Beemer's birthday. It was Halloween. We all sang "Happy Birthday" to Beemer. "Make a wish my Beauty. Our wish is for you to come home."

We felt so bad Beemer was not at home to greet all the Trick or Treaters as he always did on his birthday. When the neighborhood kids came who knew Beemer they all asked "Where's Beemer?"

"He wasn't feeling so well, but he is getting better."

"Well tell him Hi!"

"We will. Happy Halloween."

Beemer's Tale 358

After the last Trick or Treaters for the night left we went in. There was an ache in my heart. "Well Beemer is getting the biggest Birthday celebration ever when he gets home." I said to Jack. Jack nodded.

When Beemer's Doctor thought Beemer might be ready to try some food we brought beef with rice that Jack cooked and baby food.

Coming Home Again

> After a week Beemer was released. That was one of the longest weeks of our life. We were so elated when we could finally bring him home. When we got home we said "You are home my boy. You are home. Let's get you to your couch." Beemer wanted to sniff the yard a bit before going inside. We were so happy to see him lying in his favorite spot on the couch after going inside. I massaged his legs and back knowing it must have been so uncomfortable for him to lay in the cage even with blankets and padding. With lots of hugs and kisses we said "Welcome Home Beemer."

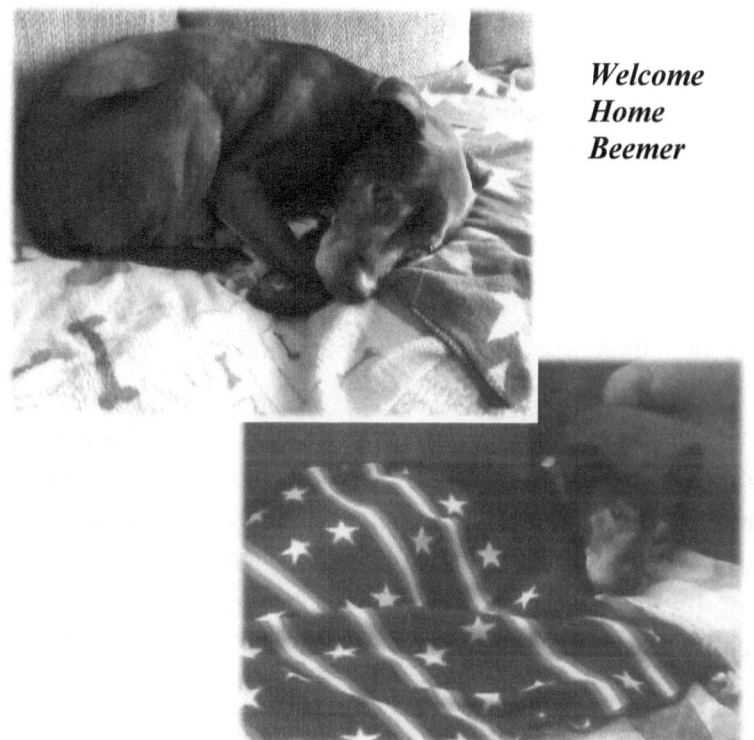

Welcome Home Beemer

After Beemer was home the neighbors came to see him. "Looking good Beemer." "So glad you are back Beemer." Friends and Family would call or text, or come by and check on how Beemer was doing.

Kasey brought Dudley by and Annie brought Winston to see him. "His tail is wagging that's a good sign." "Yes yes it is. Thanks so much for all your support. We are so happy he is home." "We are happy to see him too." "And now you really made Winston's day!" Even Jimmy our friend and Mailman was happy to see him. "'Beeeemer' Glad you are back."

When Beemer came home he had to have a very bland diet. He could only have just meat and rice and nothing with spice of any kind. Beemer was eating but not lots. He had lost 5 pounds and was down to 52 pounds. The Vet thought it would be good to continue on fluids 3 times per week until his appetite fully returned to avoid him getting dehydrated. Also it was recommended to give him small meals 5 times a day.

I worked from home on the days we had to bring Beemer in for fluids. We would bring him in on my lunch hour. The first time we went we walked in and Laurie came out. I said "Beemer there's your Laurie." Beemer loved everyone there but seemed to connect with Laurie. Laurie explained it would only take a few minutes and they would put the fluid under his skin to be absorbed. When she brought him out he had a pouch on his back. I was so upset. "Oh my poor Beem. You okay by boy?" "Don't worry it does not hurt him at all. The fluid will absorb in a few hours. Plus this is the first one so his skin is tight. Next time it will not be so much." I was shocked. It reminded me of the Hunchback from Notre Dame. "Really don't worry." She assured us. Sure enough after a few hours the fluid was absorbed. This was better than Beemer having to stay there and be on a slow IV drip like when he had his hospital stay. When we brought Beemer most of the time it would be Laurie or Beemer's right hand man as we called him Jason. Jason showed us how to check if Beemer was dehydrated so we would know just in case if we had to bring him in sooner or more often.

We were so very grateful to everyone at the Vet who took such good care of him. We can never thank them enough for all they did for Beemer. Beemer has been going there his whole life and they take such good care of him. They are the best and more than we could ever ask for.

After a few weeks we noticed on the Vet bulletin board that someone advertised to make home pet visits for shots or whatever was needed. It turned out we knew who it was. It was Charlotte whose husband Jeremy was good friends with our friend Ken. We had met both Charlotte and Jeremy several times at parties at Ken and Sandy's house over the years. And Charlotte's sister Macey worked at Beemer's Vet which we knew for years and had no idea of the relation. It was another one of those life connections.

"This is perfect." I said to Jack.

"We should definitely call her."

We called Charlotte and set it up for her to come Monday, Wednesday and Friday. It was perfect so Beemer could just be at home and did not have to keep going in. It was great to see Charlotte again as well.

When Charlotte would come Beemer would reluctantly jump off the couch. Jack set up an IV pole from one of his video camera stands and Charlotte would give Beemer his fluids. It took about 5 minutes. He stayed there so patiently. As soon as he was done he would do a shake. I would sing "Shake it off like Taylor Swift Shake it off." Charlotte laughed.

It was also helpful in case I had to go into work I did not have to reschedule Beemer's appointment as that was so important for him. Beemer was definitely doing better and it really helped him. Again we felt so fortunate to have seen Charlotte's card on the bulletin board.

While all this was going on with Beemer Jack's Mom had also been in and out of the hospital at the same time. We were running around with trying to make sure both Beemer and Jack's Mom were getting the best care possible. Both Beemer and Jack's Mom spent their birthdays in the hospital. We have a great appreciation for everyone at Beemer's Vet, all the

Beemer's Tale 362

Doctors and the Hospital workers as we got a small dose of what they do every day while we were nursing Beemer and Jack's Mother back to health at the same time.

When Charlotte came Christmas week to give Beemer his fluids we bought her presents from Beemer. "Aww that is so sweet. Thank you. Thank You Beemer. Wait till I tell my husband I got presents from Beemer. We'll see what presents he brings for Christmas." Charlotte told us how her husband helped her wrap the presents last year for their two children, a son and a daughter who are adorable. He signed all the gifts from him. We laughed so hard.

While Beemer was getting back on track we started slowly and went on shorter walks. We would drive him to the park and let him walk there. We missed seeing all the people we know at the stores and on the way to the park when we would walk to the park but we still got to see them when we went to buy something. Beemer would be in the car and they often came over to say hello to him. We still did get to see all the regulars at the park when we are there. Even though our walks were shorter I would say "You are doing Fantastic my boy."

We are always so proud to be with Beemer. Every time we are out and someone stopped and to ask about him we "Beem" with pride.

Vet Visit – Beemer's Puppies

On our follow up visit with Beemer after his hospital stay everyone at the Vet came over to see us that day.

"Did you see the puppies?" Emma said "You have to see the new puppies. They look so much like Beemer. We are calling them baby Beemer puppies."

"Aww really? We would love to see one." I said.

Emma went to get one and brought a little boy puppy back snuggled in her arms. "They are only 5 days old."

"Oh how absolutely adorable. Look Jack." I lightly touched his back. The puppy was so soft. His eyes were not even open yet. Beemer just raised his head and sniffed gently.

"Beem he looks like you." I said.

"He does look like him being black and with the white spot on his chest. Some even have white on their feet." Emma said.

"We never got to see Beemer as a puppy as we got him at 6 months." I replied.

"Well know you have." Emma said with a smile.

Jack and I joked "Beem your parents must still be around." Sometimes I wished Beemer hadn't been neutered when we got him. It would have been wonderful to have real Beemer puppies since he has such a special personality and is so handsome.

Baby Beemer Puppy

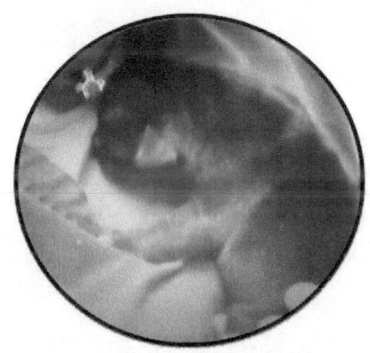

Beemer's Tale 364

When Beemer had his hospital stay with Pancreatitis we were so afraid we were going to lose him. It was really scary. We could not even comprehend the thought of being without him. It was so hard with him being at the hospital and not at home every day. It was so quiet and we missed him all day. We felt so grateful, happy, lucky and overwhelmed with all the help and support from the Doctors and Techs, God, St. Frances and the powers that be that Beemer recovered.

Chapter 23 – Reward and Retirement

There is a saying that "Every one life touches so many." That is true of Beemer. Every day of his life he brings smiles and laughter and comfort to so many. We are so grateful we are able to be a part of and experience that positive energy.

Another quote "Laughter is the best medicine." I believe this in my heart. That is my way to help others and deal with stressful situations. To make jokes and see my Mother, Gerry, Joey and many other friends and strangers in time of need to laugh and smile even for a moment. I can never repay Beemer for all the times when I would bring him for a visit and feel his calmness and genuine sweetness that he brings to them.

All the things we learned, all the wonderful people we meet, all the people Beemer helps, all the fun times we have all because of Beemer. Beemer makes it a Celebration of Life and Connections.

Beemer's Tale 366

Celebration of Life and Connections

Writing Group

I have been a member of a writing group at the Library for over 15 years. The group meets twice a month. We follow Natalie Goldberg's idea of "Writing Down the Bones" where we write on a topic for ten minutes. The leader of the group usually brings topics but anyone can suggest a topic. Then the members of the group can share or pass. Everyone usually always reads. There is no critique just sharing. We all agree it is our Writing Therapy group and we all look forward to meeting.

We have a core group of people who always come. We have become so close over the years. We feel like we know more details about one another than our own families. Sometimes we get new members who come and go for awhile and others who come every so often. We laugh and sometimes we cry, but it is always a good time.

When looking back through my journals I found many many times where I had written about Beemer. The core group knows Beemer very well and have even met him at Parades and Park events.

The following are a few of the topics.

9/17/2015

Write a Letter Thanking Someone For Being a Good Friend

We don't always take the time to say a special thank you to those who mean so much to us. I don't think I ever thanked you so I want to say thank you thank you for all you have done over the years. You have always been there for me. You have seen me when I am up and when I am down. When I laugh and when I cry. You are a shoulder to cry on and the one to make me smile when I may not feel like smiling. You have helped so many others by bringing a smile to their faces; young and old - all ages. The first time you met my Mom I will never forget. You walked right over and put your head in her lap like you knew her all your life. I don't think I ever told you thank you and how special that was. Thank you for that. I am so lucky to have you in my life and grateful for you every day. There is no one like you Beemer. Thank you and I love you.

When it was my turn to share with the writing group I said to myself – 'Hang tough.' I got three quarters through and started to tear up while I was reading. I finished as I realized it was really important to thank him. As soon as I got home I ran in and saw him on his favorite spot on the couch. He lifted his head not realizing I was home already. I sat down and kissed him on his head and said "Beemer - Thank You – For Everything". Then I gave him a big hug.

1/7/2016

<u>Describe a Wonderful Gift</u>

After seeing first hand so much loss by fire and flood to the point of having nothing but the clothes you are wearing your idea of gifts change. Don't get too attached to possessions. It could be gone tomorrow. Gifts are not just tangible gifts but there are gifts of actions, faith or talent. One of my greatest gifts would be my four legged guy – Beemer. He gives the gift of a smile wherever he goes and spreads cheer for all from old to young. When we are doing our Pet Therapy visits it truly is amazing how much it means to the patients. They light up and would move and reach and lift their arms to pet him. To share their stories of their past pets and to get that big smile. Priceless. I heard on the news they are even using Pet Therapy at colleges to calm the students during exams. How wonderful. Most wonderful gift for me – Beemer and the gift of giving.

One of the members said "Beemer – that is such a cute name. Really different."

"Yes just like him. We have the shelter to thank for his name."

Beemer's Tale 370

Greatest Gift - Beemer

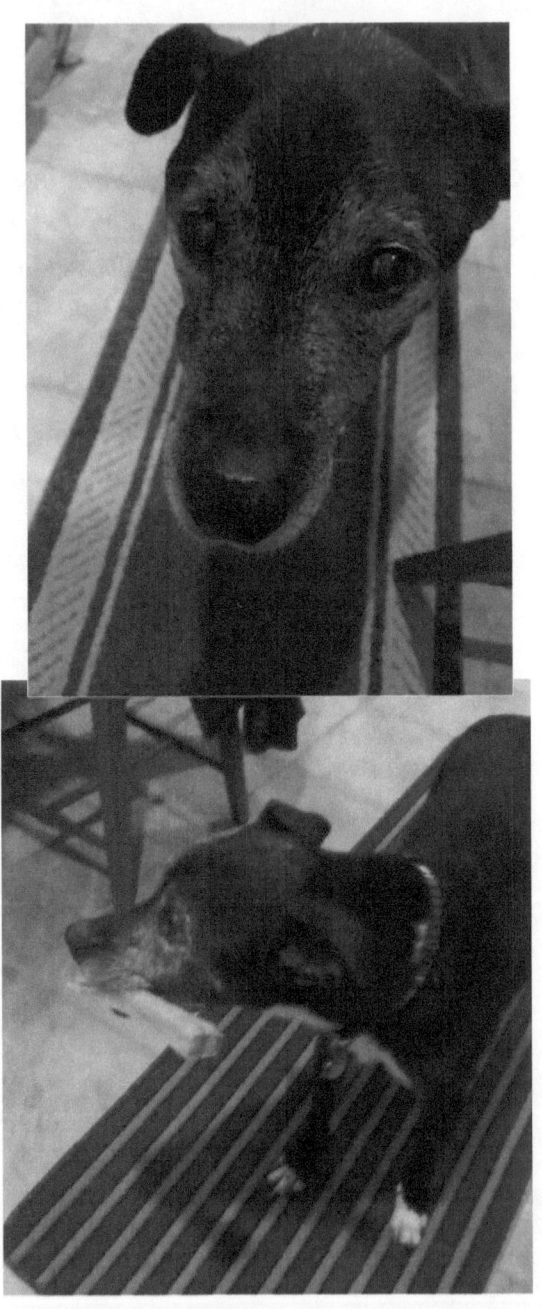

1/5/2017

<u>One Magical Moment</u>

This was my Christmas wish to have one magical moment to fix my Beemer – Let him get hungry and eat eat eat. Pig out even like we all do at Thanksgiving, Christmas and all the Holidays. I believe I believe I believe I tell myself. To have a magical moment again like when we were kids hoping Santa would bring that special present because we were so good all year. Well I think I was really good all this year. LOL. And so was Beemer. Come on Santa.

>*We made Roasts and Bacon and Filet Mignon*

>*We made Burgers and used Special Plates,*

>>*Anything we could serve him on*

>*Not a Bite he would take*

>*I even tried Cake*

>*Santa skipped my Christmas wish this year*

>*But do not fear*

>*Ronald McDonald arrived*

>*Beemer ate a Quarter Pounder and Fries!*

Once our ten minutes are up each person reads their writing. When it was my turn and I finished reading everyone laughed.

"Did he really eat that?" Kay asked.

"Yes he really did. We were so happy for him to eat anything and lucky for us they were 2 for 5!"

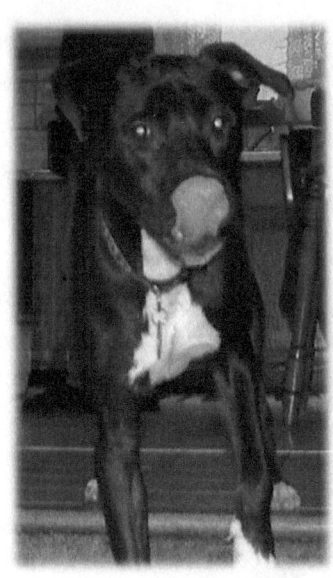

Beemer after enjoying McDonald's

Retirement

Every November we had to renew Beemer's certification for Pet Therapy visits with the agency. After Beemer's Hospital stay we decided it was time for Beemer to officially retire as a Therapy Dog and for Beemer to enjoy his time every day. He had served for 13 years and we are very proud of him.

As Beemer's owner and handler for 13 years, we learned firsthand together what an invaluable service and genuinely rewarding experience Pet Therapy is. Dogs want a purpose, a job and a routine. Beemer has them all.

We sent an email to the Agency that we would not be renewing his Certification this year.

Sent: Sunday, November 06, 2016 9:24 PM

Subject: Renewal - Retired

Dear Agency,

Our beloved Beemer has just turned 15 - it is time for him to retire and enjoy life.
He has been a Therapy Dog since 2003 - 13 years.
We have truly enjoyed all our visits and bringing a smile and touching the lives of so many.

Thank you for all your support over the years.

All the best for all your good work for Therapy Dogs.

Sincerely,

Louann and Beemer

Date: Monday, November 07, 2016 11:55 AM
Subject: RE: Renewal - Retired

Hi Louann and Beemer- Thank you for all the work you both did. Enjoy your retirement Beemer.

Best,
Patty

Beemer's Tale 374

We loved every minute of our Therapy Visits. We think Beemer did too. We felt like we were really doing something so positive and impacting to help others. We are so lucky as we have a Pet Therapy visit every day living with Beemer. If you had a bad day you could kiss him and hug him and feel better. At the end of the day we would snuggle in bed and feel each other's warmth and comfort. We have lost many loved ones, both family and friends over the years. Beemer is there to support us through it all. Thank You Beemer. You truly are our 'Sun Beem'.

Beemer Snuggling in Bed

It's Beginning to Look A Lot Like Christmas

While shopping for Christmas presents I saw this stuffed Gingerbread Man with a big smile. He was 2 foot long. I thought it would be so perfect to give it to Beemer for Christmas. We thought when he was done playing with it he could use it as a pillow. We caved and gave it to him early before Christmas. It was the biggest toy he ever had. Beemer looked so funny trying to pick him up. Beemer ended up standing him up between his paws and the Gingerbread man was taller than Beemer's head. We took pictures. After a few days the Gingerbread Man is now Beemer's new pillow.

Beemer with his Gingerbread Man

Beemer's Tale 376

Snowball

I was in the local Hallmark store near our house and I saw these light up snowballs. They were white soft fluffy balls but if you threw them or dropped them they would light up. They were the coolest. I bought a bunch of them thinking that it would be so fun to get them for everyone as a surprise. I brought them home and they were in a handle bag. As I walked in I placed the bag on the floor so I could greet Beemer. "Beem. How are you my boy?" I said as I saw him on the couch. He did not fly off the couch as quickly as when he was younger, but he did come over and of course had to sniff the bag. I gave him hugs and kisses. I had left the bag on the floor and had not yet moved it. Later after dinner we saw Beemer go over to the bag. He gently took out one of the snowballs out of the bag. Since I left it on the floor he must have thought they were for him. "Jack look. Aww he's so adorable." I did not have the heart to take it away. "Beem you got your own snowball!" Once I said that he knew it was his and he got so excited like he did whenever he got a new toy. He trotted over and jumped up on the couch with his snowball. He began to chew and bat it with his paw. We watched him and laughed as the snowball kept lighting up. The next day I went back to the store to get a replacement for Beemer's. I never even thought he would want one. I should have known better. Now Beemer had his own snowball for Christmas.

Last year I had bought this beautiful red velvet bag that said Merry Christmas and had a white satin ribbon on top just like Santa Claus has. At the time I had no idea what I would do with it but hey it was 50 percent off so I bought it. Turned out it had the perfect purpose.

While Beemer was still recovering we hosted for any Holidays, family gatherings, parties and birthday celebrations. They all understood and were happy to come.

Christmas Day arrived and everyone came to our house as it was harder for Beemer to travel. After our wonderful Christmas dinner it was time to open presents. I had put all the snowballs in the red velvet bag. I hid Beemer's snowball behind his pillow on the couch. I picked up the bag and threw it over my shoulder. "Ok everyone close your eyes and you will get your first gift. I am going to bring the bag around and everyone has to reach in and pick a present. Keep your eyes closed until everyone gets one." I went to each person and they reached in the bag. Beemer was hanging out on the couch watching. It was interesting seeing everyone's reaction as they did not know what they had but it was soft and fuzzy. After I got to the last person I then went to get Beemer's snowball from behind the pillow and handed it to him. "Okay open your eyes." Everyone looked at what was in their hand. I then yelled "Snowball fight." Jack knew ahead of time what I had planned so Jack and I threw ours; his at my nephew and mine at my sister. Everyone caught on fast and joined in the fight. We were all laughing and picking up the snowballs and throwing them again over and over. "This is awesome!" my nephew chimed in. Beemer jumped off the couch trying to catch them all. Too much fun! The snowball fight was definitely a success.

Servicemen

One day while walking in the park a large man was walking toward us. He stopped to ask about and pet Beemer. I said my usual response "His name is Beemer. He is my teenager. He is 15 and is a retired Therapy Dog."

"Nice." he replied as he was patting Beemer gently on the back. "Well I know how you feel buddy and what it's like to be on the bench. I was in the military."

"Oh wow." I smiled and said "Thank you for all *your* service."

He just nodded and said "Have a good day."

"You too." I looked back as the man was walking away and whispered "and God Bless."

Chapter 24 – Walk On

One day we were walking in the Beach Park and there was a lady walking with a cane. As we got closer without prompting or a request Beemer walked right up to her. He was in Pet Therapy mode. "Hi. It's okay he is friendly." I said to make sure the lady would not be concerned. She replied "Hello – who is this handsome one? He is older I see." "This is Beemer. Yes he is 15. He is my teenager and is a retired Therapy Dog." As she bent over to pet Beemer she told him "Thank you for your service Beemer. You did a great job." "Thank you so much. Yes he really is a wonderful guy. We are so very lucky." She petted him for another minute and then straightened up. "Have a great day." I said. As she started on her way she replied "You too and you too Beemer."

After Beemer came home from the hospital, neighbors and friends all ask how Beemer is doing.

"He is actually doing better. He is holding his own." Or

"He is doing great thanks." would be our response.

"So glad to hear." "He is in our thoughts." Or "We were praying for him." they would say.

"Oh thank you so much!" It truly meant a lot to us.

As we walked by our neighbor Cathy's house, she was outside getting groceries out of her trunk. She turned and said "Hi." I waved and said "Hi. We are going slow, but we are going."

Beemer's Tale 380

Cathy smiled. I remember the days when Beemer and I would run by Cathy's house and wave 'Hi' as we sped by.

Just the other day we were walking down our street and we saw another neighbor. He was getting out of his truck. His Mother was not doing so well. We walked over.

"Hi how are you doing? How is your Mother?"

"Just waiting for the call."

"Oh. I am so sorry. It is so hard even though we know it is coming." His eyes started to tear up.

I hugged him and said "I totally understand." And I did as we were in a similar situation with Jack's Mother. My eyes were also tearing up. Beemer just stood the whole time patiently waiting for us to continue our walk.

He then bent down to pet Beemer. "How you doing buddy?"

"He's hangin in like all of us." I said trying to smile. "Love you." I said and gave him a big hug. As Beemer and I walked away I thought Beemer just gave a Pet Therapy Visit and Beemer didn't even know it or probably he did.

Beemer still loves going to the park and we go every day barring bad weather. In a small way he is still doing Therapy Visits as everyone he meets in the park comes over and smiles and pets him, hugs him and asks about him. "You still got it kid."

Beemer is a beacon of hope and inspiration. He has come so far from where he started. Beemer serves and touches so many lives. In our minds Beemer is truly a gift from Heaven. He is a kind and gentle soul to everyone – Friends, Family, Neighbors, Strangers and All Animals.

In whatever time we have left every good day is a gift. Every day we get to go to the park is cherished. It makes me think of the song Jerry Lewis always sang at the end of the Labor Day Telethon.

So Beemer, Jack and I "Walk On" and at the age of 15 Beemer still brings smiles to everyone he meets.

Post Author's Note

Everyone believes their pet is the greatest and they should. They are such an integral part of your life. They are with you from morning till night; sharing your life in both happy and sad times.

There are the ones though that stand out and have a special gift. Beemer is one of them. I can say that as I am not totally biased as he was not ours originally. I saw something in him. Always knew Beemer was different even before he was ours. We were lucky enough for him to become ours. Beemer was the first one that I considered mine as all the others I have cared for were someone else's.

Every one of these heartwarming stories with Beemer is true. With Beemer we did not have to imagine or make anything up. It is just how he is. Anyone who knows him will tell you how special he is. So it is important to treasure all the good times with your loved ones every day.

Timeline – Highlights

2001

- **October – Beemer is Born**
    - We picked Halloween – **October 31, 2001**
        - **Happy Birthday Beemer! So glad you were born!**
- **Beemer is found by the side of the Road with a broken leg and brought to the shelter.**

2002

- **April 13 – Beemer Adopted from the Shelter**
    - **Beemer finally has a new home!**
    - **Description/Stats**
        - Lab/Pit Mix, Black and White
        - Likes Kids, Playful, Friendly, Loveable
        - Weight 39.8 lbs.
- November 16 – Coming Home
    - Awesome Day! Beemer Came to Live with Us.
    - Beemer has his Forever Home.

2003

- **January 18 - Fenced in Yard for Beemer to Run Free**
- **May 11 - Beemer's First Bark**
- **May 15 – Beemer Foster's Lucy**
- **Training**
    - **January** – Attended some Basic Obedience classes with Beemer to observe and then signed up for next session

2003 Training Continued

- **April - June 7** - Basic Obedience – Graduate – 8 week course
  - **Description/Stats**
    - Lab/Pit Mix, Black and White
    - Likes Kids and Other Animals, Playful, Friendly, Loveable
    - Weight 45 lbs.
- **June – August** - Beginner Intermediate | Canine Good Citizen – Graduate – 7 week course test included
  - Pre-requisite: Basic Obedience
- **September – November** – Therapy Training – 8 week course and AKC test
  - **Description/Stats**
    - Lab/Pit Mix, Black and White
    - Loves Adults, Kids and All Other Animals, Playful, Friendly, Loveable, Calm, Gentle
    - Weight 50 lbs.

- **September 27 - Beemer's First Block Party**
- **October 26 - Beemer's First Halloween Parade**
- **October 31 – Beemer's First Birthday Party!**
  - **Trick or Treat visitors**
  - **Steak Dinner and Ice Cream!**
- **Degrees Earned**
  - **November 15** - American Kennel Club – Canine Good Citizen Test
  - **November 26** - Certified Registered Therapy Dog By Agency

- **December 2003 to January 2004 – Beemer Starts Agility**
    - "Intro to Agility" Training – 6 weeks
        - Training was indoors – total confidence builder

<u>2004</u>

- **January 2004** – "Intro to Agility" Training – continues
- **February - March** – Agility – "Beginner #2 Agility" Training – 6 weeks
    - Great to have indoor exercise during winter
    - **Description/Stats**
        - Lab/Pit Mix, Black and White
        - Loves Adults, Kids and All Other Animals, Playful, Friendly, Loveable
        - Weight 55 lbs.
- **April 2004 to September 2006** – Agility "Drop-In" – Weekly
    - Went as often as schedule available for exercise not competition
    - **Fun and Class Clown**
    - **Developed Allergies** ☹
- **June 2, 2004 – Beemer Started Barking!!!**
- **November 26, 2003 to November 6, 2016** - Certified Therapy Visits
    - 13 years of helping countless people
    - **Description/Stats**
        - Lab/Pit Mix, Black and White
        - Loves All Adults, Children and Animals, Playful, Friendly, Loveable, Calm, Gentle, Sweet and Kind
        - Weight Range: 55 -60 lbs.

- - -
    - Various Assisted Living and Nursing Homes in area
        - Mom's Facility and many others
        - Fashion Shows
        - Howl-O-Ween Parade Oct 2010
        - Yappy Valentine's Day! Feb 13, 2011
        - Windward Beach DogFest on Sunday, September 18th in Brick. The attire is "Patriotic" and we would love to have you join us and show off our wonderful therapy dogs! The Fest runs from 11:00 - 4:00 and the show can be scheduled for 11:30.
    - Neurological Center – April 2009 - July 2012
    - Home Visits
        - Jack
        - Gerry
        - Mom
        - Jeanne and Lily
- **Dog Walks for Cancer**
    - Stadium September 11, 2011

2005

- **Continued Agility and Pet Therapy**
- **March 21- April 20 - Lived with Sam during House Construction**

2006

- **Continued Agility and Pet Therapy**
- **February - Beemer Developed Allergies** ☹

2007

- **Continued Pet Therapy**
- **January 6 – Beemer's Polar Bear Plunge**

- **June - Beemer Moves to His New House**
- **September 9 – Dog Walk for Cancer**

2008 - 2010

- **Continued Pet Therapy and Dog Walk for Cancer**
-
- **January 24, 2010 THERAPY REFRESHER Course**
    - Back by popular demand, this 2 hour course is a lot of fun, instructional and a real solution to the winter blues.
    - We design games, there is problem solving and social skills are renewed.
        - Was so fun to see everyone again!

2011

- **Continued Pet Therapy and Dog Walk for Cancer**
- **Hurricane Irene – We Need a Boat**

2012

- **Continued Pet Therapy and Dog Walk for Cancer**
- **Hurricane Sandy – Lights Out**

2013 - 2015

- **Continued Pet Therapy and Dog Walk for Cancer**
- **March 12, 2014 – Beemer's Operation**
- **March 27, 2014 – Beemer's Stitches Out**

2016

- **Continued Pet Therapy**
- **October 28 - Beemer Hospital Stay** ☹
- **November 1 - Beemer Home Again** ☺
- **November 6 - Retired Certified Therapy Dog**
    - Notified the Agency of Beemer's Retirement
        - Still got it!!!

Beemer's Tale 388

- o **Description/Stats**
    - Lab/Pit Mix, Black and White and Distinguished Touch of Gray
    - Loves All Adults, Children, and Animals, Playful, Friendly, Loveable, Calm, Gentle, Sweet and Kind
    - Weight 53 lbs.
- **Just Keep Walkin!**

Tribute

On February 21, 2017, a sunny 45 degree day, our beautiful boy Beemer went to Heaven. With the window open and the sun on his back our Angel flew to the Rainbow Bridge. There you can run like the wind again our Beauty, lightning fast like you used to do. For sure we will meet you at the bridge when our days are done. Thank you for your beautiful life. We love you Always.

I wrote the ending of the book before Beemer's passing. I wanted to leave it that way as Beemer was always a positive energy and to give hope for all.

We went everywhere together, walked for miles and greeted everyone we met with a smile and a tail wag. And when Beemer could no longer go we had everyone come to us including Family Gatherings, Holidays, Parties and Birthday Celebrations. They all understood and were happy to come. Daily family, friends and neighbors would call, text, walk or come by and check on how Beemer was doing.

Beemer you gave us so many wonderful memories. Beem – thank you for them all! We were always so proud to be with you Beemer. Every time we were out and someone stopped and asked about you I would "Beam" with pride.

Till the very end you were a trooper so loyal and true. I can never repay you or be grateful enough for you and how you enhanced and made a difference in my life.

Beemer's Tale

One life that meant so much to so many. One can only hope to make a positive difference in the world. Beemer in his short time here definitely did.

When someone or something is your focus and an integral part of your life every day for 15 years and then is gone it leaves a big hole in your heart. Beemer we planted you a garden in your yard near the statue of St. Francis where you used to lay. You will Forever be in Our Hearts.

Here is my dream and vision of the Afterlife. I will make my way through the field toward the Rainbow Bridge. Beemer comes running toward me. I drop to my knees and open my arms wide as we would always do when we went to Agility. Beemer will whiz by me because he is so fast and then circle around and run into my arms. That one moment of seeing him again running toward me will be Heaven. I laugh. I cry. I kiss him and hug him tight. I tell him I love him.

When I looked though my writing journals I saw I wrote about you Beemer a lot over the years. Now I write to the world so they know about you.

Media Post – 2/24/2017

Rest in peace beautiful boy. You can run like the wind again and be well. Thank you for your beautiful life. You were a kind

Beemer's Tale

and gentle soul to everyone - Family, Friends, Neighbors, Strangers and All Animals. You served countless people in need for 13 years. You were truly a gift from Heaven. We will meet you at the Bridge when our days are done. We love you Always.

Media Post – 2/21/2018

A year ago today we lost our "Best Boy in the World and Handsomest Guy in Town" as we always told you our Beautiful Beemer. On all our car rides you were always our "Wingman". You have earned your "Wings" Beauty. We Love and Miss you every day. Thank you for your Service to Others and being the Joy in our Life every day for 15 years. We were so very Lucky and Privileged to know one such as you Beemer. One of a kind. Once in a lifetime. Priceless.

Hope you are enjoying all your days as you so Deserve and "Walk On" until we see you again.

Acknowledgements

First we have to thank God for giving us the wonderful gift of Beemer. He is definitely a gift from Heaven.

Want to say a special thank you to all of Beemer's Trainers over the years as they truly helped Beemer become the special guy he is.

We cannot thank enough our Dear Doctors, Techs and Staff who take such good care and being there for us and our beloved Beemer. We feel so lucky to have all of you. Your expertise, thoughtfulness and caring ways could never be replaced. We truly appreciate all you do to help so many; you all have such a special gift. We feel you are part of our family.

Thank you to Beemer's Pet Therapy Agency for all their support for 13 years.

Sincere and heartfelt thanks to all of our friends, family, neighbors, Pet Therapy patients, and strangers who were touched by Beemer and loved Beemer as much as we do. A sincere thank you for all the Cards, Flowers, Cookies, Soup, Kind Words and Thoughts sent by so many. We love you all.

One of Beemer's best buddies was Jack the Cat. When Beemer passed away Jack's little girl drew a beautiful picture of Beemer and she said "Even Jack is sad." It was very special.

And a sincere thank you to all those who help rescue animals, provide health care, adopt pets from shelters and those who do Pet Therapy. You are the everyday heroes. You may not make it in the news but you are the stars and make a difference in the hearts of animals and people every day.

Thank You.

BEEMER

www.ingramcontent.com/pod-product-compliance
Lightning Source LLC
Chambersburg PA
CBHW021828220426
43663CB00005B/167